FOREIGN

INVESTMENT

ADVISORY

SERVICE

Using Tax Incentives to Compete for Foreign Investment

Are They Worth the Costs?

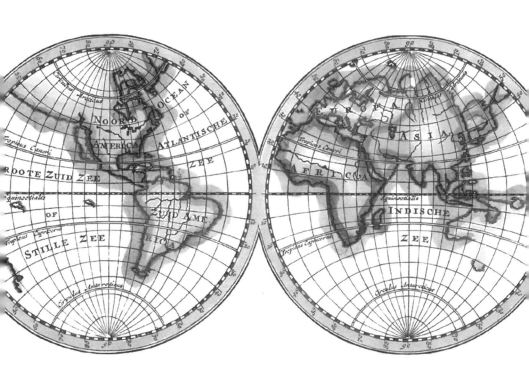

OCCASIONAL

PAPER

15

Louis T. Wells, Jr.
Nancy J. Allen
Jacques Morisset
Neda Pirnia

© 2001 The International Finance Corporation
and the World Bank,
1818 H Street, N.W., Washington, D.C. 20433

The International Finance Corporation (IFC), an affiliate of the World Bank, promotes the economic development of its member countries through investment in the private sector. It is the world's largest multilateral organization providing financial assistance directly in the form of loans and equity to private enterprises in developing countries.

The World Bank is a multilateral development institution whose purpose is to assist its developing member countries further their economic and social progress so that their people may live better and fuller lives.

The cover design is based on an antique map by an unknown artist.

Library of Congress Cataloging-in-Publication Data

Using tax incentives to compete for foreign investment : are they worth the costs? / Louis T. Wells, Jr. . . . [et al.].
    p. cm. — (Occasional paper / Foreign Investment Advisory Service ; 15)
    Includes bibliographical references.
    ISBN 0-8213-4992-9
    1. Investments, Foreign. 2. Tax incentives. 3. Investments, Foreign—Indonesia. 4. Tax incentives—Indonesia. I. Wells, Louis T. II. Series. III. Occasional paper (Foreign Investment Advisory Service) ; 15.

HG4538 .U855 2001
332.67′3—dc21   2001045464

Contents

iii

Figures and Tables

TAX HOLIDAYS TO ATTRACT FOREIGN DIRECT INVESTMENT: LESSONS FROM TWO EXPERIMENTS

Figures

Tables

v

HOW TAX POLICY AND INCENTIVES AFFECT
FOREIGN DIRECT INVESTMENT: A REVIEW

Table

Foreword

This volume consists of two essays, one by Louis T. Wells, Jr., and Nancy J. Allen and the other by Jacques Morisset and Neda Pirnia. Both essays are on the use of tax incentives to attract foreign direct investment, and are thus complementary. The Wells and Allen essay presents results of their original research, while the Morisset and Pirnia paper surveys the research of others on the same topic.

The problem of whether and how to use incentives is among the most important but least heralded issues facing national and regional policymakers throughout the world. Incentives can be direct subsidies (including cash payments or payments in kind, such as free land or infrastructure) or indirect subsidies (tax breaks of various sorts or protection against competition from rival firms, including import protection, for example). To be considered an investment incentive, however, a tax break must not be available to all investors but, rather, must be tailored to specific investors or types of investors. Thus, for example, accelerated depreciation offered to all investors would not be an investment incentive in the sense used here, even if accelerated depreciation might benefit certain specific investors—those operating in highly capital-intensive sectors—more than others. In developing countries, tax incentives are especially common, and they may be aimed at foreign direct investors and not available to domestic investors.

There are many arguments made for offering foreign investors investment incentives in general and tax incentives in particular, but most of these arguments can be boiled down to two categories: first, it is argued that incentives will increase the total flow of new investment; that is, investments will be made that would not be made in the absence of incentives. Second, it is argued that if governments of locales that are alternative locations for foreign investors offer incentives, then the government eager to ensure that it gets the investment must match those incentives or face the prospect of losing investment to the competing territories. This might be true even if the investor would, in the absence of any incentive, make the investment somewhere in the region. Thus, in somewhat more abstract terms, the two general arguments are as follows: first, incentives increase the aggregate of foreign investment available to developing countries; and second, incentives can affect the spatial distribution of investment, even if the first argument does not stand up.

The main arguments made against investment incentives can also be boiled down to two. The first is that incentives have little, if any, effect on the total foreign investment that is made worldwide, and thus in the aggregate, incentives create a net transfer from taxpayers (or, in the case of indirect subsidies such as protection from imports, from consumers of the relevant product) to investors. In the case of foreign investors in developing nations, this transfer is primarily from a poor country to a richer one. The second argument is that even if the first argument does not fully stand up (that is, because incentives do increase the total investment worldwide), the cost to the public of incentives exceeds the additional benefits that are created by the investment that would otherwise not occur.

Analysts who support these arguments against investment incentives maintain that even if incentives do affect the spatial distribution of investment, the answer is not for governments to compete with one another in offering incentives (an "everyone loses" proposition) but, rather, for governments to establish agreements among themselves not to offer incentives at all. They may even agree to eliminate tax incentives unilaterally, since their costs are so high.

The first essay in this volume explores these issues in the context of Indonesia. The Indonesian government has offered tax incentives to foreign investors during some periods of recent history, but incentives have not been available during other periods. Thus, the country offers a "natural experiment" for testing which of the arguments outlined above stand up and which do not.

The results mostly support the arguments made *against* incentives. In particular, the authors find little evidence that when Indonesia eliminated tax incentives, there was any decline in the rate of foreign direct investment into the country. They note that this is true even though other governments in the same region continued to offer incentives. Thus, it would appear that neither of the arguments made in favor of tax incentives holds for Indonesia. Not only did the availability or nonavailability of tax incentives fail significantly to affect the aggregate investment coming to Indonesia, but it does not even appear that the ending of incentives caused investors to shift their investments to countries where governments continued to offer incentives. (It is important to note that when Indonesia first ended tax incentives, this was done in the context of a general tax reform whereby corporate income taxes were reduced across-the-board. In the absence of this tax reform, as acknowledged by Wells and Allen, elimination of incentives might indeed have reduced investor enthusiasm for locating projects in Indonesia. This leads to the important qualification that in the case of Indonesia, the nonavailability of tax incentives seemed to have little effect on the flow of foreign direct investment given the existence of an overall tax regime that offered corporate tax rates that were in line with international norms.) If Indonesia's experience with incentives is generalizable, it follows that many governments can safely afford to withdraw incentives unilaterally, without fear that this will drive desired foreign investment to other locations.

Wells and Allen buttress their findings with very persuasive calculations showing that even if tax incentives lured some foreign investment into Indonesia that might otherwise not have come, the costs to the Indonesian taxpayer were far in excess of the benefits of the additional investment. Indeed, under plausible assumptions, they find that the net cost of incentives to the Indonesian treasury may have exceeded the total additional investment Indonesia received. In fact, the costs of incentives, this essay suggests, go beyond the direct loss of tax revenue from investors who would come anyway, and include efforts by firms to manipulate transfer prices to reduce taxes in taxable activities, higher taxes for others, and general erosion of the tax system through perceptions of unfairness. One stark conclusion that follows is that incentives can result in net balance of payments outflows, if tax savings are remitted abroad—a perverse result indeed. Even if such an extreme result does not occur, however, Wells and Allen provide convincing evidence that tax incentives are not at all cost-effective.

Given this, why did Indonesia reintroduce tax incentives? The research suggests several reasons, based on an analysis of internal government documents. First, there is an agency problem created by bureaucratic and institutional factors within the Indonesian government: the government bureau that administers incentives (the Badan Koordinasi Penanaman Modal, or BKPM) is responsible only for drawing foreign investment into the country and not for the costs of doing so. The BKPM thus faces no incentive, nor indeed any responsibility whatsoever, for administering its programs in a cost-effective manner. Second, there is the power of a good story, even if the story isn't true or is a special case. In particular, while hard evidence does not support the belief that Indonesia has lost any significant amount of foreign investment to other nations in the region because these other nations offer better incentives than does Indonesia, it is nonetheless widely believed in Indonesia that there are major cases of "lost" investment. While such stories abound, close examination reveals that most of these stories are not wholly factual and are rarely typical. Rather, they often amount to the equivalent of "fish stories" ("you should see the size of the fish that got away"). However, the stories are even believed by persons at senior political levels in the government. Finally, policymakers act out of frustration. It is difficult to deal with the real problems that keep investors away: political and economic instability, corruption, and red tape. It is easy (though costly) to pass a new law to offer more incentives.

This essay should certainly be read by anyone who has an interest in Indonesia and its current economic plight. At the time of this writing, Indonesia was under great pressure to do something to change course or face increasingly dire consequences. What Wells and Allen contribute is an important analysis that argues that tax incentives for foreign investors are *not* part of the answer to this plight and, indeed, may actually be counterproductive, especially if restoration of these incentives were to become an excuse for not implementing deeper and more difficult reforms.

More important, the essay is essential reading for officials of other countries that are eager to attract foreign direct investment. Other countries are likely to find tax incentives for foreign investors as unsuccessful and as costly as did Indonesia. If, as one suspects is the case, Indonesia's experience is not unique, these policymakers may want to reexamine their own tax incentives, asking whether they are fulfilling the objectives that they are meant to serve. Especially important, officials might consider whether some sort of regional or global collective action might be in their interests: for example, a call for a World Trade Organization obligation to limit selective incentives, as is done in the European Union, or to ban them altogether.

As noted in the introductory paragraph, in the second essay in this volume, Morisset and Pirnia provide a review of earlier literature pertaining to the same issues discussed in the first essay. They show that the results of other research are generally consistent with the findings of the research in Indonesia, notably that tax incentives neither affect significantly the amount of direct investment that takes place nor usually determine the location to which investment is drawn. Studies have used two wholly different methodologies, that is, surveys of investors and econometric tools. With respect to the former, one striking finding reported in several surveys is that there is a large discrepancy between the way investors view tax incentives and the way government officials view the same incentives; surveys of investors tend to rank incentives quite low as determinants of investment, while studies using econometric tools rank them high.

There are some important qualifications, however, that emerge from the literature. The effectiveness of incentives may differ among types of investors or investments. Location choices for "export platform" foreign direct investments are more likely to be affected by tax incentives than are those for foreign direct investments meant primarily to serve local domestic markets. Yet Wells and Allen point out that export-oriented foreign investment in Indonesia grew particularly rapidly after tax holidays were eliminated. Similarly, tax incentives may have a significant impact on location decisions within a genuine single market, such as within the European Union. Incentives may also affect location decisions when investors are choosing among locations that are approximately equal in terms of other factors that may affect their choices. In fact, sometimes equivalence in location and single market may combine to make incentives particularly attractive for one economic entity (nation or locale), even if they do not increase total investment flows. Thus, Alabama may be forced to offer incentives to match those of Mississippi for investors serving the national market or maybe the area in the North American Free Trade Agreement. Indonesia, on the other hand, should probably not respond in kind to Singapore's tax incentives. One might also speculate that certain types of investors who offer services for which the precise location of "production" is vague or of little importance might seek to locate at least some investment in "tax haven" countries. Certain financial services and perhaps electronically based services may be examples.

Also, Morisset and Pirnia suggest that in evaluating the effects of tax incentives, account must be taken of home country policy (where "home country" means the nation from which the investment originates). One reason that tax incentives might be ineffective as a determinant of location of investment is that some home country policies offset the tax savings created by the incentive. As a practical matter, such offsets result when the home country taxes income of its investors on a worldwide basis and rejects "tax sparing" provisions in treaties to avoid double taxation. The United States does so; hence one might expect that U.S. investors would be relatively indifferent to the offer of tax incentives when deciding whether to invest in a particular country. Some other countries, by contrast, tax only the domestic income of their residents or agree to tax sparing arrangements. There is, in fact, some econometric evidence to suggest that in making foreign investment location decisions, investors domiciled in countries with the latter practices do indeed respond more positively to tax incentives than do investors based in the United States. On the other hand, Indonesia's experience suggests that home country policies matter less than one might expect. Although Japanese investors (whose Indonesian income was covered under tax sparing arrangements) complained regularly about the elimination of tax holidays, they still flocked to the country. In fact, Indonesia gained over its neighbors in the competition for Japanese investment, even without tax incentives.

Taken together, these two essays provide a basis for much more sophisticated analysis by policymakers than has been typical in the past. The result ought to be serious questions about the ratio of benefits to costs of tax incentives that are offered to investors. The essays also raise questions about government institutional arrangements that create serious agency problems with respect to tax incentive policies, as well as efforts to reduce costs of incentives by increasing administrative discretion in awarding them. Moreover, I hope that a result will be more interest in international agreements to limit tax incentives; the result of limits would almost certainly be beneficial to developing countries.

Edward M. Graham
Senior Fellow
Institute for International Economics
Washington, D.C.

Tax Holidays to Attract Foreign Direct Investment

Lessons from Two Experiments

Louis T. Wells, Jr.
Nancy J. Allen

Acknowledgments

Part of the research for this essay was financed by the Harvard Institute for International Development.

The authors benefited from comments by Timothy Buehrer, E. Montgomery Graham, Yasheng Huang, Robert Kennedy, Jacques Morisset, Debora Spar, and Joseph Stern on earlier drafts of this essay.

Acronyms and Abbreviations

ASEAN	Association of Southeast Asian Nations
BKPM	Badan Koordinasi Penanaman Modal (The Investment Coordinating Board)
HIID	Harvard Institute for International Development
IMF	International Monetary Fund
NPV	Net present value
OECD	Organisation for Economic Co-operation and Development

1

Introduction

In the 1970s and early 1980s, Indonesia offered foreign investors tax holidays that were similar to those granted by many other countries at the time, and today. In a dramatic turnaround in 1984, however, Indonesia became one of the very few developing countries to eliminate tax holidays. The results of this "natural experiment" support the broad conclusions of research elsewhere: tax holidays do not determine the location decisions of many foreign investors. The findings are significant, especially in light of the rough estimates that one can now make of the costs of tax holidays. A comparison of the effectiveness of tax holidays in attracting investors with their costs supports the argument that, for many countries, costs outweigh benefits.

Yet, in spite of the experience showing that tax holidays were not efficient ways to attract foreign investors, pressures continued for Indonesia to offer tax incentives. Those pressures eventually led to the reintroduction of tax holidays in 1996; this time, however, they were administered under a different scheme, one often recommended as a way of lowering costs. This second natural experiment, and experience elsewhere with similar discretionary systems, suggests that they are not likely to be successful in many countries.

The 1996 tax holidays were soon dropped, but new incentives appeared in 2000, when the country was desperately trying to attract investors—as the effects of the Asian economic crisis continued. Indonesia's experience helps to explain the persistence of tax holidays in spite of their seemingly high net costs, and suggests policies that could reduce their drain on the resources of developing countries.[1]

2

The First Experiment: Eliminating Tax Holidays

Early Tax Holidays in Indonesia

The base for the first natural experiment was created in 1967, when Indonesia began to offer a number of incentives to attract foreign direct investors. At the time, proponents of incentives argued that they were necessary to attract investors to the country, which had been closed to foreign investment in the first half of the 1960s under President Sukarno. Tax holidays, it was claimed, were all the more important in light of the country's high corporate income taxes (60 percent, under the 1925 Company Tax Ordinance) and dividend withholding taxes.[2] As a result, the 1967 investment law[3] exempted foreign investors from corporate income tax for a period of up to five years and from dividend withholding taxes on those profits even if they were remitted later. Once the basic tax holiday expired, the applicable tax rate for foreign firms could be reduced up to 50 percent for an additional five years.[4]

The first law applied only to *foreign* investment. As has happened in many other countries, however, this limitation was soon lifted. A 1968 law authorized tax holidays for *domestic* investors as well.[5]

Professor Mohammad Sadli, who headed the original implementing organization (eventually known as Badan Koordinasi Penanaman Modal, or BKPM), explained that it was only "fair" to offer as much or more to domestic firms as foreign firms received.[6] Also, there was a belief that incentives to domestic firms would bring back capital that ethnic Chinese had parked offshore.[7] In 1970, the original foreign investment law was amended to bring the incentives for foreign and domestic investors to virtual par.

The 1967 law said little about standards for awarding tax holidays, mentioning only "priority sectors"; but the implementing organization soon developed a set of criteria for awarding the incentives to make them more predictable to investors:

■ If investment in the first two years was more than $2.5 million and the project saved or earned foreign exchange, it would receive a three-year exemption from corporate and dividend tax.

■ An additional year would be given for such investment if it was outside Java, in infrastructure, or considered especially risky.

■ Additional incentives could be granted for investment made in the years 1967 and 1968 if it was "pioneer" or for more than $15 million.[8]

As a result, although the law allowed considerable discretion to those administering it, in practice discretion was largely in terms of evaluating whether or not a project was risky.

Three years later, an amended law incorporated criteria into the legislation itself.[9] Tax holidays were to be granted by the minister of finance (who delegated authority to the investment agency, where the ministry had a representative) rather automatically, according to the following rules:

■ A basic tax holiday of two years was granted to all firms in priority sectors.

■ An additional year would be awarded to projects that significantly saved or earned foreign exchange.

■ An additional year would be provided for large or risky projects (in practice, apparently over $1 million in the early years).

■ An additional year would be provided for projects located outside Java.

■ An additional year would be granted to projects that carried "special priority" status.

In total, a project could receive tax exemptions—from corporate income tax and from withholding taxes on dividends[10]—for up to six years. The clock on holidays started running when commercial production commenced (a date to be certified by the director general of taxation, in the ministry of finance).

The criteria for awarding incentives reflected contemporary beliefs about the kinds of investments desirable for development. Professor Sadli explained that the size criterion, for example, was based on the belief at the time that large firms were the ones that had the technology Indonesia wanted for development, and that smaller investments should be left for Indonesian firms. Moreover, the country was especially eager to attract large companies because investments by them would show their confidence and thus attract other investors.

Although the legislation authorized (as opposed to mandated) tax holidays for projects that met specified criteria, in practice incentives were granted to any firm that qualified and whose project was licensed. There was no attempt to determine whether the investor would come in the absence of tax incentives.[11]

The criteria for incentives were clarified and modified somewhat over subsequent years. In 1977, for example, the investment agency classified industries into a number of categories: those open for investment and designated as priority, those open for investment with incentives, those open for investment but without incentives, and those closed for investment. This rather detailed classification removed still more discretion in granting tax holidays. With only small adjustments, the system remained essentially the same until 1984.[12]

The End of Tax Holidays in 1984

The first natural experiment was launched in 1984.

By the early 1980s, some of the original arguments for tax holidays were losing their persuasive power. Since several name investors had established themselves in Indonesia, the need to attract some firms as role models had disappeared. Because the corporate tax rate in Indonesia had fallen to 45 percent[13] and treaties for the avoidance of double taxation had lowered dividend withholding taxes for many foreign investors, the argument that high taxes had to be offset had lost its strength. As a result, when Indonesians began to plan a dramatic tax reform, the need for continuing tax holidays became a hot issue in internal discussions of the ministry of finance.

It was soon decided that the corporate tax rate would be further lowered, to 35 percent, in line with rates that were appearing in a number of other countries (Gillis 1985).[14] As part of the research accompanying reform proposals, financial projections for projects submitted by foreign investors were examined; the resulting report concluded that, on average, internal rates of return for investors would not differ greatly under a 45 percent tax rate with five years' holiday and a 35 percent tax rate with no holiday.[15] Thus, dropping tax holidays would make most investors no worse off than they had been with holidays.

Further, reformers were aware that empirical studies in Indonesia and elsewhere were showing that tax holidays played only a relatively minor role in foreign companies' decisions about where to place new investment.[16] They also argued that taxation of worldwide income and foreign tax credit systems in some home countries meant that tax holidays in Indonesia led to larger tax payments to investors' home countries: "reverse foreign aid," as these payments became known in the ministry of finance.[17] It was also pointed out that the holiday system introduced distortions across sectors and classes of firms, favoring large investors, a class that policymakers were no longer so eager to encourage.[18]

Although research on tax holidays and debate within the government had focused on the benefit side of incentives, opponents of tax holidays were beginning to grasp the cost side. Officials in the ministry of finance recognized that incentives imposed costs on the treasury, in terms of direct revenue costs and also administrative problems, but no effort was made to quantify those costs,[19] and no formal calculations compared benefits to costs.

Even strong opponents of tax holidays recognized that there were probably cases in which incentives might indeed influence investment decisions, but they feared that allowing any tax holidays would dangerously open a path to revenue leakage. Incentives would go to firms that would come anyway, and tax holidays would be pushed for other purposes.[20] Better to lose a few investments if that was to be the price of avoiding high-cost incentives in the future.

In spite of the arguments of reformers, opposition to eliminating tax holidays was strong. Many officials (especially outside the ministry of finance, where the cost side weighed in heavily) argued that foreign investment in Indonesia would drop sharply without special incentives that matched those of neighboring countries. Further, supporters of continuing tax incentives picked up a new argument: the earlier liberal requirements on domestic partnerships had given way to restrictive policies following 1974 demonstrations, which had attacked foreign, especially Japanese, "dominance" of the economy. Tax holidays, proponents argued, helped to offset Indonesia's domestic ownership requirements.

Although evidence was not always available to test the claims of the two sides, in the end the reformers won: tax holidays were eliminated for investors approved after 1983, while other incentives (tariff exemptions, guarantees, and so on) remained intact. In promoting the change, officials presented the lower corporate tax rate of 35 percent as an "incentive to *all* investors," substituting for incentives to a special few, the costs of which had to be borne by others in the form of higher tax rates (Gillis 1985, p. 237).

The natural experiment had been set in motion. The results would help settle questions concerning the benefits of tax holidays.

The Impact on Foreign Investment

The year 1984 proved difficult for the reformers. The first data available after tax holidays were dropped strengthened the conviction of those who viewed the new policy as a major mistake: foreign investment approvals declined from those of the previous year. Jeffrey Winters described the time as one of "widespread alarm" (1996, p. 173).[21] Almost immediately, domestic and foreign pressures emerged for reconsidering the decision to drop tax holidays. Insinyur (engineer) A. R. Soehoed, who had run the investment agency from 1973 to 1978, attacked the reformist economists and advisers on the issue, for example.[22] One foreign writer said, "But it would appear that a large number of potential investors still consider the tax holiday a very important incentive," and went on to suggest that it be restored (Harink 1984, p. 8).[23] Even President Suharto was, it seemed, deeply concerned (Winters 1996, p. 184). Yet the reformers held to their resolve.[24]

Soon, recovery of foreign investment inflows supported the original optimism of the reformers. The return of foreign investment is clear in figures 1 and 2. Figure 1 shows both the number and value of projects approved each year from 1978 to 1993.[25] Figure 2 reports the logs of the number and value of projects for the same period, to make it easier to compare growth rates before and after the elimination of incentives.[26]

Statistical tests of the differences between growth rates before and after 1984 confirmed what the figures graphically show. Consider the crudest tests first. If one examines the values of foreign investment, the rate of growth from 1978 through 1983 was slightly higher than that for 1984 to 1993, but the difference between the growth rates in the two periods was not significantly different from zero. On the other hand, if the comparison is based on the number of projects approved, the growth rate after the end of tax holidays was slightly higher than that before; again, the difference between the two growth rates was not significantly different from zero. [27]

Figure 1. Foreign Investment Approvals in Indonesia, 1978–93

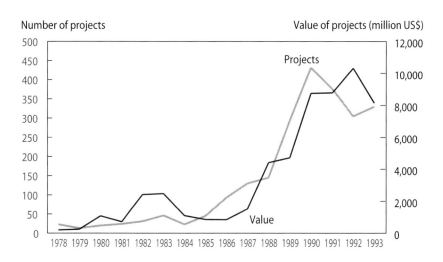

Figure 2. Logs of Foreign Investment Approvals in Indonesia, 1978–93

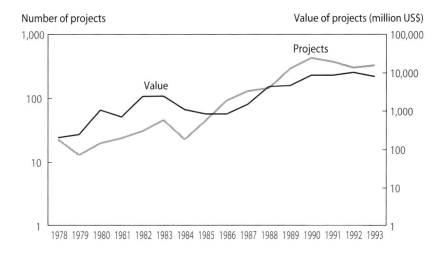

To test the robustness of the findings, we adjusted the numbers in various ways. For example, similar tests were made on the figures without including a very large refinery project that was never implemented. The handling of the transition years 1983 and 1984 was adjusted: first, by averaging the number of projects and the values for those two years (see below for reason) and then, by eliminating the two years. Whatever the adjustments or combinations of adjustments, the conclusions held. The differences between growth rates in investment with tax holidays and those without tax holidays were not significantly different from zero (for some samples of results, see appendix A).

As more encouraging data on foreign investment began to come in, explanations emerged for the low foreign investment figures for 1984. There had, in fact, been an upward blip in foreign investment approvals for the year preceding reform. Since it was widely expected that tax holidays would be reduced, a number of investors accelerated their applications for investment licenses. There was also some evidence that the investment agency had been induced to predate some 1984 approvals to 1983 (thus the adjustments we made to the 1983 and 1984 figures in the statistical tests).[28] Investors gained from 1983 approval dates, since the grandfathering of pre-1984 incentives meant they would receive tax holidays as well as enjoy the new lower tax rate.

Skeptics could still claim that the continued growth in foreign investment in Indonesia was the result of external events. Indeed, rising wages and the revaluation of currencies in Korea and Taiwan encouraged firms in those countries to increase foreign investment in a search for lower-wage sites to manufacture labor-intensive products for their export markets. Because of these and other external changes, foreign investment grew in all the low-wage countries of the region. Similarly, one could argue that the lower tax rate offset the lack of tax holidays after the reform was implemented. But if tax holidays had been decisive factors in the location decisions of investors, one would expect foreign investment in Indonesia to have lagged behind investment in other countries that continued to offer

Table 1. Average Shares of Total Foreign Investment in Five ASEAN Countries
(Percent)

Year	Country					Total
	Indonesia	Philippines	Thailand	Singapore	Malaysia	
70–84	10.8	2.6	7.7	46.4	32.5	100.0
85–90	9.2	6.9	17.0	49.3	17.6	100.0
91–96	19.8	6.5	11.7	3.8	28.1	100.0

Note: ASEAN is Association of Southeast Asian Nations.
Sources: 1970–84 data from IMF, as reported in Hill 1988, p. 48; remaining data from U.N. 1997, Annex table B.1.

tax holidays and tax rates comparable to the new Indonesian rates. As table 1 shows, however, rather than losing long-run share of foreign investment in the region, by the period 5–10 years after it had eliminated tax holidays, Indonesia had managed almost to double its share.

Another prediction could have been that the elimination of tax holidays would have different impacts on investors of different nationalities, reflecting different tax systems of the investors' home countries. Investors from countries that offer credits for taxes paid abroad might be less affected by changes than firms from countries that did not tax foreign-earned income. But it is difficult to identify any such influence of home country in the investment flows. As one test, we examined three groups of investors: (1) those from the United States, which taxes foreign-earned income but gives tax credits for taxes paid abroad; (2) those from the industrialized countries of the Netherlands, France, the United Kingdom, and Japan, which do not tax foreign-earned income or give foreign tax credits under tax sparing arrangements;[29] and (3) those from the emerging economies of Hong Kong, Singapore, Korea, and Taiwan, which probably pay no tax at home on foreign-earned income.[30]

Figures on shares of investment at the end of the tax holiday period and 10 years later show, at most, a very weak impact of the home country tax system.[31] The share of U.S. investors in total foreign investment in Indonesia went up, as one might predict, since U.S. investors benefited relatively little from tax holidays in the first place and would continue along their old path. The increase, however, was quite small. The share of U.K. and Japanese investors fell somewhat, consistent with their having benefited from tax holidays. On the other hand, the share of Dutch investors increased substantially, as did the shares of investors from Singapore and Korea (see table 2), contrary to predictions based on home country tax systems. In sum, it is hard to find evidence in Indonesia that the home country tax system had a large and consistent impact on investors' reactions to tax holidays.

On the other hand, Japanese investors lodged the bulk of foreign complaints (see pp. 27–30) about the elimination of tax holidays. This is as one might expect, given the tax sparing treaty that allowed Japanese firms to capture the benefits of any tax holidays. But in spite of the complaints, Japanese investment in Indonesia continued to grow rapidly after the tax holidays were dropped. Even domestic investment behaved much like foreign investment: it remained fairly flat until 1982, spiked in 1983, declined in 1984, and climbed thereafter, showing a pattern almost identical to that of foreign investment.

Table 2. Shares in Total Foreign Investment in Indonesia, 1967–95

Home country	1967–85		1967–95	
	$ million	%	$ million	%
United States	1,381	9.0	10,660	10.0
United Kingdom and Japan	5,249	34.1	30,472	28.8
Singapore and Korea	346	2.2	13,216	12.4
Netherlands	499	3.2	7,320	6.9
Other	7,939	51.5	45,132	41.9
Total	15,414	100.0	106,800	100.0

Note: The end years in these sources are close to, but are not identical to, those used in figures 1 and 2 and table 1.

Sources: Calculated from data in Hill 1988, table 4.2, pp. 56–57; and PUSDATA ONLINE INDONESIA–DATA CENTER in early 2001 (*http://www.dprin.go.id/data/indonesia/investment/profile.htm*).

In summary, the experiment in Indonesia provides strong evidence that a country can attract growing amounts of foreign direct investment without offering tax holidays, at least if its general income tax rate differs little from that of its neighbors.[32] Foreign direct investment in Indonesia increased over the 1978–93 period at a striking rate of about 25 percent per year compounded (21 percent for number of projects; 28 percent for value). The growth rate did not change measurably after tax holidays were eliminated, although one might have expected some slowdown in this rapid growth simply from market saturation. Indonesia's success in attracting investors without tax incentives occurred in spite of the fact that neighboring countries offered generous tax holidays. Moreover, it appears that tax holidays had little impact on the mix of investors, at least by home country. One has to conclude that investors will go to a country—if its market, climate, and policies are attractive—whether the country offers tax holidays or not.

Consistency with Findings Elsewhere

Lest one believe that Indonesia was a special case because of its large domestic market, the experience of Hong Kong is worth mentioning as well, even though its data are particularly difficult to interpret and it is quite different from Indonesia in a number of ways.[33] In spite of its small population, Hong Kong has not offered tax holidays, even though other countries in the region do. Hong Kong offered a low income tax rate to all rather than grant exemptions from taxes (and consequently impose higher taxes on other investors). With this policy, Hong Kong attracted foreign direct investment flows that, in the majority of years between 1991 and 1997, were greater than those going into much larger Asian countries, such as the Philippines and Taiwan.[34] The totals of investment entering Hong Kong have differed little from those attracted to the much larger Thailand, with its liberal incentives policy.[35]

One could argue that Hong Kong's incoming investment figures are contaminated with "round-tripping" from China and with investment coming into Hong Kong but destined for other Asian sites. Yet, even discounting for round-tripping, which might have accounted for a quarter of foreign investment,[36] and for onward investment,[37] per capita (or per unit of gross domestic product) direct foreign investment in Hong Kong has been strikingly high.

Perhaps more convincing than the Hong Kong story, however, is the fact that the outcome of Indonesia's experiment with dropping tax holidays is consistent with the findings of many empirical studies, which have concluded that tax holidays affect the investment decisions of some firms but that the overall impact is not very great. The body of research on the effect of incentives is now quite large, and has been summarized elsewhere.[38] Therefore, we will cover only the core methods and findings of the two categories into which most of this research falls.

Theoretical Research

In a stream of theoretical research, scholars have calculated the financial impact of tax holidays on the returns from hypothetical investment projects. They then assume that investors behave in simple, profit-maximizing ways:[39] if tax holidays increase the net present value of projects, they will attract more investors. Not surprisingly, researchers using this approach find that, under assumptions that make calculations feasible, tax holidays will increase the returns to investors; therefore, researchers conclude, investors will invest more in countries offering them. Researchers following this approach usually do not address the question of whether the greater investment flow to a country offering incentives is a net addition to the flows to the developing world, or whether it simply represents a diversion from countries offering smaller incentives to those offering greater ones.

In spite of the great care with which some of this research has been done, the results remain unconvincing. First, the studies do not adequately account for the complexity of the tax situation facing multinational firms. Some home country tax codes, for example, impose no tax on foreign-earned income. The tax systems of some other home countries result in a different outcome: the benefits of tax holidays in developing countries may be largely offset by increased liabilities of the parent enterprise to the tax authorities of the home governments (this can be the impact of the U.S. foreign tax credit system). In the real world of investors, the impact of tax systems such as that of the United States is very complicated. The foreign tax credits that a firm can use to offset home country taxes can depend on the extent that earnings are retained in the operations in the host country, on tax rates in other countries in which the multinational operates, on how the investment is financed (in particular, the proportion declared as debt), and on administrative choices made by tax authorities. Second, to some extent, firms that operate under more than one tax regime have ways of allocating their profits within their networks; by assigning them to minimize taxes, they make any simple calculations suspect. These kinds of problems have led most theoretically oriented researchers simply to ignore the home country tax regime. Although the omission makes the calculations easier, it sharply reduces the plausibility of the results.

Much more important, the conclusions based on calculations of projections fail to recognize the fact that actual management decisions may not reflect the calculations that academics make, no matter how carefully those calculations are done. First, many investment decisions are strategically determined, from investors' needs to diversify sources to the drive to match moves of competitors, for example.[40] Second, facing the complexities of international tax rules, managers, it seems, rarely calculate and compare all possible outcomes. Rather, there is a great deal of evidence that most managers follow "satisficing" behavior instead of profit-maximizing behavior when the various alternatives are extremely complex.[41] Rules of thumb guide decisions, not difficult and uncertain calculations.

Empirical Research

Recognizing that investors may not always respond in ways assumed by calculations, a number of researchers have tried to examine the actual decisions managers make. Some of the most frequently cited studies of this kind are econometric studies that look at the impact of differences in average or marginal tax rates in home and host countries. Using aggregate data, these studies cannot focus on incentives. Typically, they must assume that all investors in a country—or at least all in a gross category—face the same average or marginal tax rate. They usually find that lower rates in host countries are associated with larger foreign investment. One summary estimate suggests an elasticity of –0.6 (Hines 2000).[42] But they do not directly answer the question relevant for this essay: What is the impact on investment flows of changing the tax rate *temporarily* for selected investors?

In order to get at the effect of tax holidays, as opposed to differences in more generally applicable marginal or average tax rates, another category of empirical studies has looked at the incentives issue directly. These studies are based on interviews with or questionnaires to managers. The results have uncovered patterns of decisions that differ from the predictions of the optimization models.

Since researchers have to collect data directly from firms, most such work is based on relatively small samples.[43] Still, there is sufficient convergence in the findings of an accumulation of somewhat different studies that confidence can be placed in the results. When surveys ask managers to assign weights to various factors that influence their investment decisions, for example, tax incentives are usually ranked rather low. Overwhelmingly, empirical researchers conclude that tax incentives do not have a major impact on actual investment decisions.[44]

The empirical work also contains strong hints that responses of investors differ by certain characteristics of the project. The greatest consensus among researchers has developed around the importance of a project's market orientation. Tax holidays are more likely to affect location decisions for export-oriented projects than for those that serve the local market; investors in export projects see themselves as having alternative sites and thus, it seems, are more likely to make direct comparisons among countries. Also, several researchers agree that incentives are more likely to affect location decisions *within* a market area (single country or an effective free trade area) than they are when the choice is between countries that cannot be viewed as a single market.[45]

Some research suggests that industry also plays a role in the effectiveness of tax incentives (Spar 1998).[46] There is little work on whether investors' responses to incentives vary by characteristics of the host country in question (particularly, whether tax holidays matter more to investors if the generally applicable tax rate in the host country is very high[47]). Also unresolved is the important question of whether the impact of tax holidays comes from their direct financial implications for the investor or from the signal of welcome by the host country that incentives convey to hesitant investors.[48]

Still, there is a great deal of consensus in the empirical research: as the Indonesian experiment suggests, tax holidays do not determine location decisions for a large percentage of investors. Many researchers would also agree that their impact is largest when the project in question is for export, or when the decision is among sites within a single market.

3

Estimating the Costs of Incentives

Examining the effectiveness—that is, the benefit side—of tax holidays in attracting investment is not sufficient for the policymaker. Since research concludes that at least some investors are likely to be sensitive to tax incentives, the benefits associated with attracting those firms should be weighed against the costs of a tax holiday program. Yet almost no research has attempted to measure the costs of tax holidays.[49] Nevertheless, one can make some reasonable estimates of costs. Combined with the evidence from Indonesia's natural experiment and academic research, cost estimates help in deciding on rational policy.

Costs of Redundant Incentives

From the government's point of view, providing tax incentives ought to be viewed as equivalent to granting a direct subsidy, if some of the firms that receive incentives would have come even without the incentives. An estimate of the subsidy can be calculated by allocating the foregone revenue from firms that would have come anyway to the projects that would not have come *but for* the incentives.[50]

Thus, an estimate of the cost of incentives should begin with an estimate of the redundancy rate: in the simplest case, the percentage of investors receiving tax holidays who would have come even if they had not been granted incentives. If tax incentives are given only to investors who would not otherwise have come, and are exactly the amount required to attract them, then there is no revenue loss from the incentives–zero redundancy. On the other hand, if incentives go to investors who would have come anyway, there is redundancy and the foregone revenue from those redundant incentives represents a cost to the treasury. That cost is equivalent to a subsidy to attract the incremental investors.

There is likely to be an additional source of redundancy as well. If incentives to some investors whose decisions are influenced by them exceed the amount required to attract them, the increment is also a cost to the economy.

Although it is obvious that there was redundancy under the pre-1984 tax incentive scheme in Indonesia, in practice, determining the redundancy rate and calculating the costs are not easy. Estimating relationships between redundancy rates and subsidy equivalents is, however, simple. Assume for the time being that there are no excess incentives given to those investors whose decisions are indeed driven by tax holidays. In that case, let t equal the tax rate, Y equal the investor's average return, R equal the redundancy rate (the fraction of investors who would have come without incentives), N equal the number of years of tax holiday, and I equal total foreign investment Then the tax unnecessarily given up to the foreign investor is $R \times I \times Y \times t \times N$.[51]

The incremental investment attracted is $(1 - R)I$. Thus, the subsidy as a fraction of the incremental investment attracted is:

$$(R \times I \times Y \times t \times N)/(1 - R)I \text{ or } R \times (Y \times t \times N)/(1 - R).$$

Consider the following hypothetical, but reasonable, example: Say that foreign investment earns an annual profit before taxes of 20 percent on invested capital, that the corporate tax rate is 45 percent, as it was before the 1984 reform in Indonesia, and that the typical tax holiday offered investors is five years. According to the above formula, the subsidy would equal the amount of incremental foreign investment attracted, if the redundancy rate is about 70 percent. If the redundancy rate is as low as 55 percent, the subsidy is equivalent to about half of the incremental investment. These are, of course, very large subsidies by any standard.[52]

The calculations could, of course, be refined by discounting future foregone tax revenues by an appropriate rate to arrive at a net present value (NPV). A more sophisticated formula would then be:

$$\text{NPV of subsidy} = \sum_{n=1}^{N} \frac{1}{(1+r)^n} \times \frac{(R \times I \times Y \times t \times N)}{(1-R)}$$

where r is the discount rate and NPV is expressed as a fraction of the incremental investment attracted.

Appendix B provides some tables of subsidy equivalents at two different tax rates and for two different tax holiday periods. The analyst can easily calculate subsidy equivalents under different assumptions.

An effort has been made to measure the actual redundancy rate for incentives in Thailand. The researchers found that at least 70 percent of the investments that received incentives would have occurred without them.[53] If this number approximates the redundancy rate in Indonesia, the cost of tax holidays in the 1970s was about equal to the total amount of investment they attracted, according to the simpler formula.

An alternative approach to estimating redundancy is to accept Hines's (2000) figure for the tax elasticity of foreign direct investment, about –0.6. It appears that the value of a five-year tax holiday in Indonesia was roughly equivalent to a 22 percent reduction in the tax rate, since the internal rate of return for actual projects varied little between the old 45 percent tax rate with five years of tax holidays and the new 35 percent tax rate and no holidays. Applying

Hines's estimate of tax elasticity, one can estimate that the old tax holidays resulted in a 13 percent increase in foreign investment. Since practically every investor received incentives, the redundancy rate was thus at least 85 percent; in this estimate, the subsidy was greater than the incremental investment attracted.

In fact, even these figures understate the actual costs. First, some investors who are attracted by incentives are likely to receive more than the minimum needed to influence their decisions. Although almost impossible to measure in practice, the increment is a form of redundancy that imposes a cost on the treasury. Second, although redundancy rates are usually measured only for foreign investors, domestic politics usually leads to tax holidays for domestic investors as well, as happened in Indonesia. Local firms receive incentives even though it has rarely been argued that tax holidays will significantly increase domestic investment.[54] These impose an additional cost on the treasury. Third, many countries that offer tax holidays have found it difficult to end them once they have run out for a particular project. In extending holidays, officials seem to respond to investors' arguments that without an extension, their firms would face unfair competition from new investors, which would operate under tax incentives.[55] Since an extension is unlikely to affect the amount of investment, the result is to impose still another source of redundancy.

In summary, even if the few existing estimates of redundancy rates are too high by a considerable margin, the calculations suggest that the costs of tax holidays are extremely large. But there are good reasons to believe that the available calculations understate, rather than overstate, the effective redundancy rates. No doubt, if the costs of tax holidays were regularly presented as direct subsidy equivalents, they would receive much less support than they currently enjoy.

Other Costs of Tax Holidays

Even these calculations ignore other potentially important costs of incentives. While even rough estimates of the additional costs are extremely difficult to make, they arise from the facts that tax holidays erode the broader tax system and draw attention away from more effective and less costly ways of attracting investment of all kinds.

Erosion of the Tax System

Tax holidays place significant burdens on tax administration and on other taxpayers, who have to make up the lost revenue.

Tax holidays are usually granted on a project basis, rather than on a firm or business-group basis. Therefore, some parts of a business— either particular product lines or those parts located in different regions—can be subject to tax holidays while other parts bear normal income taxes. A rational manager will shift profits from the taxed activities to the untaxed entity by manipulating charges for office overhead, transfers of goods, loans, royalties, and various services.[56] In theory, tax authorities can determine "arm's length" prices and reallocate profits between taxed and untaxed parts of the enterprise. In practice, this often proves impossible. When tax administrators attempt to deal with such problems, they must use rather arbitrary rules. The result is an increased perception of red tape and lack of transparency that discourages investment. Indonesian tax officials recognized, but had no measures of, these costs in the early 1980s when they were debating reform.

Tax holidays also increase administrative problems because tax authorities usually do not monitor company books during the period in which a firm is exempt from taxes. As a result, asset purchases, depreciation charges, and other accounts can be manipulated during the holiday period to reduce reported income, and thus taxes, after the end of the holiday.

Whatever the source of leakage in tax revenues—direct or indirect—it means that the taxes of those entities not granted tax holidays have to be higher than otherwise in order for revenue needs to be met. Higher general tax rates impose disincentives on other investors and on recipients of incentives once tax holidays have expired. To the extent that taxes influence investment decisions, the result may be less investment in nonsupported activities. Moreover, differential tax rates—low on investments with incentives and correspondingly high on others—further the feeling among taxpayers that the tax system is unfair, encouraging taxpayers to manipulate the allocation of profits and to cheat on reporting gains.

Diversion of Attention

Perhaps even more important, the ease with which incentives can be granted imposes still another cost: policymakers tend to ignore the more difficult reforms that will have a larger impact on foreign investment. These include relaxing constraints on investors (for example, closed industries, domestic content requirements, domestic ownership requirements), reducing bureaucratic barriers, remedying deficiencies in infrastructure, and so on.

Once the crutch of tax holidays disappeared in Indonesia, productive debate about the investment climate grew; as a result, a number of changes were instituted to promote investment, both domestic and foreign. The "Deregulation Package" of May 6, 1986, began the liberalization of imports, exports, and investment. In particular, domestic ownership requirements were gradually relaxed (in 1989 and 1992), approval procedures were simplified and accelerated, more sectors were opened to foreign investment, and new approaches to easing imports for export-oriented firms were introduced. Broader deregulation made it easier for both foreign and domestic firms to do business in Indonesia and signaled a general opening up of the economy.[57]

4

The Pressures for
New Tax Holidays

In spite of the evidence suggesting that tax holidays are not very effective in attracting foreign investment, developing countries have hardly abandoned them; in fact, it seems that incentives are increasing rather than declining.[58] In Indonesia, pressures for reintroducing tax holidays continued even after investment recovered and evidence accumulated that they were not necessary to attract large inflows of foreign capital. The sources of those pressures help in understanding the actions of policymakers elsewhere.

Pressures to restore tax holidays in Indonesia began almost immediately after they were dropped in 1984. Insinyur Soehoed, for example, remained unconvinced by the data, and said: "In reality, tax holidays are highly relevant in generating enthusiasm among investors. . . . The problem was with the board of directors of the parent company that owned the investing company. For them, the availability of a tax holiday was a deciding factor on whether to invest in a country or not. If there were no tax holidays, then they simply would not come here to invest" (BKPM n.d., p. 108).

Since ministers of finance were particularly concerned about new tax incentives, they typically asked their advisers to prepare analyses when new proposals for incentives emerged. As a result, the memoranda in the files of the Harvard Institute for International Development's (HIID) advisory group in Indonesia provide useful data on the origin and frequency of proposals for restoring tax holidays.[59]

■ August 1986: HIID prepared a memorandum in response to a Japanese paper on Indonesia's investment climate and the lack of tax incentives.[60] The memo pointed out that the amount of Japanese investment approved in 1985 was the largest since 1976; the lack of special tax incentives must not be a huge problem. The memo also challenged the way data were used by the Japanese author. Another memorandum in the same month responded to a study done by Coopers and Lybrand that compared incentives in the region and showed Indonesia to be deficient.[61]

■ May 1987: An HIID memorandum responded to more complaints by Japanese firms; again, it pointed out that Japanese investment had continued to grow rapidly, especially in export-oriented projects, and that Japanese investments in Indonesia were larger than their investments in any other ASEAN (Association of Southeast Asian Nations) country.[62]

■ October 1987: A memorandum responded to proposals from Ginandjar Kartasasmita, the head of the investment agency for new incentives. His proposals were apparently made in response to a report titled "1987 Comparative Investment Incentives,"[63] and to new requests by Japanese investors, who claimed that Indonesia was not competitive with other countries, such as Thailand (Buehrer 2000).

■ November 1991: Another memorandum on tax incentives was prepared, but it is not clear what stimulated the request.[64]

■ May 1993: A memorandum addressed another set of proposals from the investment agency, for a return to a basic two-year holiday plus supplemental holidays for certain types of projects.[65] The proposal called for an additional year of holiday each for net foreign exchange-earning projects, large projects (over $10 million for domestic projects, over $50 million for foreign ones), or 100 percent equity financing. An additional 20 percent tax credit was requested for all expenditures for human resource development and high technology.

■ April 1996: A memorandum addressed new proposals for incentives, which ended up breaking the ban on tax incentives (see chapter 5 for the second experiment with tax holidays).[66]

Pressures for the restoration of tax holidays in Indonesia were similar to those that have led to holidays in other countries. We believe that there are at least six reasons for the pressure:

1. Struggle for bureaucratic power and agency problems. Often, pressures for tax holidays have come from a country's investment authority, as happened in Indonesia. There are several reasons for this: first, the investment authority is charged with promoting investment but not with collecting revenue. If tax holidays attract any investors at all, the authority benefits; on the other hand, the costs are carried by the ministry of finance and not "charged" against the performance of the investment agency. Second, an investment institution seeks power and is likely to survive only to the extent that it has control over something of value to investors.[67] In Indonesia, the elimination of tax holidays removed one of the sources of power for the investment agency. The reforms of the 1980s and 1990s that lowered tariffs further challenged the agency's strength; they reduced the importance of its control over the Master List that specified duty-free or reduced-duty imports. A restoration of tax holidays, under the agency's control, would have made for a more influential investment authority.

2. Hidden nature of costs. Tax holidays are often attractive to bureaucrats because the costs are not easily measured. Although tax holidays amount to subsidies, they are not paid out as such, but comprise income foregone. Thus, although ministries of finance are reluctant to give tax holidays, they prefer them to cash subsidies.

3. Relative ease of instituting tax holidays. Creating an environment that is attractive to investors is not an easy matter. It is difficult to build political or economic stability by decree or by law.

Moreover, countries find it hard to reduce red tape. Market size is a given, at least for the medium term, and domestic politics may constrain the implementation of other policies that are attractive to foreign firms. Political crises, such as the one Indonesia faced in the late 1990s and early 2000, are especially difficult to remove. On the other hand, it takes little more than a stroke of the pen to introduce tax incentives, as Indonesia eventually did when foreign investment fell off in response to the crisis. Policymakers feel that they are at least doing something.

4. Company interests. Managers will ask for incentives, whether they influence the decision or not. But the tax sparing treaty between Japan and Indonesia allowed Japanese investors to reap the full benefits of any tax holidays they would receive. It is little wonder that Japanese companies usually led investors' demands for the restoration of incentives.

5. Power of individual stories. Stories of investors who "got away" seem to have an inordinate impact on decisions.[68] In the early 1990s, two specific events built strong support for a return to tax holidays. A number of Indonesians were concerned about the underdeveloped state of the electronics industry in the country, especially in light of Malaysia's success. Officials recognized that something had gone wrong in the early 1970s, when a few semiconductor firms had located in the country and then left.[69] Their concern intensified when managers from an important multinational firm approached the Indonesian government in the early 1990s with proposals to locate a very large export-oriented electronics plant there. Company managers, however, claimed that Indonesia would have to offer incentives, including tax holidays, that matched or bettered those offered by other countries in the region, if it wanted the project.

In the end, the electronics firm did not locate in Indonesia but added capacity to an existing plant in another Southeast Asian country. People close to the company report that the firm never had any intention of investing in Indonesia, but wanted an offer from Indonesia to use to improve terms in the country where it had already decided to place the investment. Nevertheless, many Indonesian officials continued to believe that the country had lost the project because of the lack of incentives. In Indonesia and probably elsewhere, policymakers and even their advisers seem to have been strongly influenced by similar cases of investments that were lost, or at least seemed to be lost, because incentives were not large enough.[70]

6. Keeping up with the neighbors. Arguments in favor of tax holidays are often phrased in terms of remaining competitive with neighboring countries. In fact, in the years immediately after tax holidays were abolished in Indonesia, pressures for restoration were frequently accompanied by data on holidays offered by other Southeast Asian countries. In Indonesia, international accounting firms were commissioned to provide data to buttress the case. The argument, of course, ignored the rapidly growing flows of investment to Indonesia after tax holidays were dropped, as well as the success of Hong Kong, with no tax holidays.

5

The Second Experiment: Discretionary Allocation of Incentives

In 1996, the accumulating pressures in Indonesia led to a second natural experiment because tax holidays were restored, but under an administrative system that differed sharply from that of the earlier regime.[71]

Although Indonesia's "no tax incentives " policy had held for 10 years, the dam began to leak in 1994. In November of that year, a new regulation allowed tax incentives for firms in certain business sectors (seemingly intended for plantations and mining) and in remote areas (meaning eastern Indonesia and three "growth triangles").[72] The new incentives, however, did not include exemptions from corporate income tax; they were limited to accelerated depreciation and longer loss carryforward. At the same time, new pressures for incentives came from negotiations with Exxon for what was billed as a huge investment to develop the Natuna gas fields in the South China Sea. The company's request for special tax terms was championed by B. J. Habibie, then minister of technology. A presidential decree was issued, this time customizing the income tax regime for Exxon's subsidiary, Esso Exploration and Production Natuna, Inc. The corporate income tax was reduced for this firm to 30 percent from the then-statutory rate of 35 percent, and the withholding tax was reduced to 5 percent.[73]

By 1996, the dam holding back tax incentives broke wide open, when a presidential decree was issued to reinstitute tax holidays.[74] Technically, the decree called for the corporate income tax to be "borne" by the government, but the results were simply tax holidays on corporate income and dividend withholding taxes.[75] The new tax holidays could be for a maximum of 10 years, starting from the completion of project construction, but not later than 5 years from approval.

The 1996 regulation and subsequent decree reintroducing tax holidays did not designate the industries or locations that would be eligible for the new incentives. Rather, they named a "Team for the Study of Tax Facilities for Certain Industries," which was to make recommendations to the president, who would then select the industries that would be eligible. Eventually, a second decree amended the team makeup and labeled it the "Team for Tax Facilities." It was made up of the coordinating minister for economy, finance, and development supervision, as chair; the coordinating minister for production and distribution, as deputy chair; the state secretary; the minister of finance; the minister of industry and trade; and the state minister for mobilization of investment funds, who was also chairman of the investment coordinating board (BKPM).[76]

Although the case for these new incentives had been argued largely in terms of helping eastern Indonesia or building the electronics industry, the incentives that emerged did not, in fact, respond explicitly to either of these goals. Long holidays could be granted to projects on Java (electronics or not). Although an additional two years could be granted for projects outside Java and Bali, the incremental nature of incentives for off-Java projects makes it hard to argue that they were primarily to benefit remote regions, and the data indicate their ineffectiveness. Moreover, only one firm that received tax holidays was to manufacture electronics.

In practice, the implementation of the first 1996 incentives differed sharply from the approach of 30 years earlier, and herein lies the reason why they provide lessons for other countries. Under the new arrangements, incentives were to be awarded on a project-by-project, or ad hoc, basis rather than according to somewhat automatic and transparent criteria. Although a list of eligible industries eventually appeared, there was no automatic entitlement to incentives even if a project did fall into one of those sectors.

In general, the ad hoc approach to awarding incentives has some strong supporters, who argue that authorities can identify firms that would not invest but for incentives and that they can calculate the amount needed to induce the investment.[77] As a result, the ad hoc approach offers an opportunity to reduce the redundancy rate, and thus the cost of incentives.

In spite of the theoretical advantages of the ad hoc approach, Indonesia did not gain from the new method. It appears that the president made the choices without recommendations from the Team. In fact, one former member of the Team told us that he could not remember that the Team ever met.[78] Although the authorship of the list of eligible industries was never made public, in 2000 the general assumption was that the list had been created by the president himself, primarily to reward firms whose owners were close to him. There is no evidence of any effort to turn to economic or business analysis.

The list of six projects that were granted tax holidays under the 1996 decree is revealing:[79]

1. PT Kiani Kertas, granted 10 years of tax holiday, is a pulp and paper plant in Kalimantan, of the Kalimanis Group, and owned by Mohamad "Bob" Hasan (a close business partner with Suharto). It became connected with a scandal when it received financial assistance from a fund supposedly dedicated to reforestation.

2. PT Trans-Pacific Petrochemical Indotama, receiving six years of tax holiday, is an olefins and aromatics petrochemical plant in East Java, and part of the Tirtamas Group, of Hashim S. Djojohadikusumo

(involved in various power, banking, and chemical projects). He is a son of former Finance Minister Sumitro Djojohadikusumo and the brother-in-law of Ms. Siti Hariyadi, a daughter of then-President Suharto.

3. PT Texmaco Perkasa Engineering, with eight years of tax holiday, is a textile industry plant in Central Java controlled by Marimutu Sinivasan (who was "chummy" with Suharto[80] and declared a suspect in a Texmaco corruption case by the attorney general's office[81]).

4. PT Polysindo Eka Perkasa, with five years of tax holiday, makes polyester products in West Java, and is related in ownership to Texmaco.

5. PT Smelting Co., with seven years of tax holiday, is a Japanese-U.S. copper smelter in East Java, processing copper from Freeport of Irian Jaya.

6. PT Seagate Technology Sumatera, with nine years of tax holiday, would have been an American-owned plant that would have manufactured electronics components in North Sumatra.[82]

The incentives to the four domestic firms became very controversial; it was widely believed that the firms received benefits only because of their connections with then-President Suharto, and certainly not because the incentives were necessary to induce investment (Industry 1997). Of the six recipients, only the last two were foreign investors and could be considered pioneer, in that no other project in the country was in a similar activity.[83] According to one former member of the Team, it was "appropriate" to give incentives only to these two.[84] Thus, the redundancy rate remained at a minimum of 75 percent.[85]

The results under discretionary allocation of incentives suggest that a highly discretionary approach may be doomed to failure in a country like Indonesia. Charles Oman, at the Organisation for Economic Co-operation and Development (OECD), describes the problem very tactfully: "Policy competition raises the delicate question of how to ensure the accountability of government officials, particularly those involved in the negotiation of discretionary incentive packages, and points up the need for governments to be able to monitor their own use of incentives" (Oman 2000, executive summary). Indonesia's experience with the discretionary system has been described more bluntly by Indonesians themselves. When the tax holidays were withdrawn in 1998, under International Monetary Fund (IMF) pressure, after Habibie became president, the head of the investment agency said that the incentives were the result of "corruption, cronyism, and nepotism."[86]

Indonesia's experience is perhaps an extreme example of what happens when incentives are granted by administrative discretion, but it is far from unique. A study of tax incentives and other subsidies granted by various states in the United States also concluded that *but for* rules were not followed; subsidies were not limited to firms that would not have made investments but for the subsidies (Hinkley and others 2000).[87]

Four problems often accompany discretion. The first is straightforward: corruption, or direct political influence by particular firms. The second is political pressure by domestic investors as a whole. Few countries can get away with awarding incentives to foreigners that local investors do not receive, but incentives are unlikely to increase investment by local firms. The third is the inherent difficulty of evaluating investors' motivations. Almost all investors will ask for incentives; why not? It is, however, devilishly difficult to tell which would not come if no incentives were granted. The fourth is the resulting agency problem. If discretionary tax incentives are awarded by some kind of organization that specializes in investment, an agency problem remains, since the investment organization is rewarded based on some measure of the amount of investment it attracts, but the costs of incentives are usually carried by others.

In conclusion, discretionary systems for awarding incentives seem not to be very successful in lowering the costs of tax holidays. Moreover, they have disadvantages: prospective investors find it difficult to forecast what incentives they will receive. Thus, they have to incur costs, in the form of conducting feasibility studies, providing other information to officials, and negotiating with decisionmakers before they can predict the outcome. The incentives, as a result, are probably less effective in attracting a very hesitant investor than are those administered under predictable, transparent rules.[88]

6

Coda

The introduction—and demise—of discretionary tax holidays did not end pressures for new incentives in Indonesia.

As mentioned earlier, negotiations for the Natuna gas fields in eastern Indonesia had interested B.J. Habibie in the possibilities of using incentives to attract more investment to poorer parts of the country. Since he had led the development of the special zone of Batam Island, which had attracted export-oriented investors, the idea of zones with special rules was not new to him. As a result, a new presidential decree created "Integrated Economic Development Zones" and allowed a number of incentives. Among these were certain exemptions from value-added taxes and sales taxes, accelerated depreciation, longer loss carryforward periods, and a 50 percent reduction in income tax. The length of the partial tax holiday was not specified in the enabling decree.[89]

The original fears of the supporters of the 1984 tax reform had materialized. Their reluctance to allow tax incentives, even in those unusual cases in which there might be strong arguments for them, came from their fear that allowing some incentives would lead to an unending stream of demands. Indeed, once the ban was broken, a flood of proposals for incentives followed. Perhaps only the intervention of the IMF blocked immediate and rapid expansion of incentives.

Still, more incentives were to come. As the economic and political crisis that began in 1997 continued, pressure mounted from the president and from Rizal Ramli, an outspoken economist and then-head of the rice stabilization agency (BULOG). HIID records show another memorandum, in September 1999, prepared in response to the new proposals for incentives.[90] Then in May 2000, President Abdurrahman Wahid instructed ministers to provide additional incentives for investors, and Rizal Ramli argued publicly that incentives were necessary to offset political uncertainty.[91] There were still doubters, even in the business community. In response to Rizal's remarks, an editorial in an Indonesian business magazine argued that the lack of tax incentives was not the problem; rather, it was the political and security conditions, and tax holidays would not help much.[92] Nevertheless, in June 2000, an amendment to the tax law was announced that replaced the controversial 1996 tax holidays with an investment allowance, accelerated depreciation, and longer loss carryforward.[93]

7

Conclusions

The results of Indonesia's experiment with dropping tax holidays in 1984 proved consistent with the findings of many empirical researchers: tax holidays do not influence the decisions of many foreign investors. Foreign investment continued to grow at a high rate without tax holidays; they were clearly not necessary for Indonesia to generate substantial inflows of foreign investment.

Still, there is no doubt that tax holidays influence the decisions of some investors some of the time. A system that grants tax holidays to broad classes of investors, however, provides incentives to large numbers of investors who would come anyway, leading to high costs for the country's treasury. If the government could identify those investors who would not come but for tax holidays and grant incentives only to them, then costs could be lowered. Yet, discretionary systems charged with awarding tax incentives only to such investors have often failed, as they did in Indonesia and, it seems, in the United States.

As pointed out, there are strong indications in empirical research that the locations of export-oriented projects are more likely to be influenced by tax holidays than are those of projects producing for the local market. Nevertheless, export-oriented investment boomed in Indonesia after tax holidays were dropped.[94] If, however, export projects are more sensitive to tax holidays than are other investments, redundancy rates may be reduced if a country can grant tax holidays only to firms that export, retaining the advantages of nondiscretion but choosing appropriate criteria. But the rules of the World Trade Organization will soon prohibit such targeted incentives as "subsidies" to exports; the exception will be for the poorest developing countries.

Redundancy rates can also be reduced if tax holidays can be limited to foreign investors, and not be given to domestic firms. Yet, few countries have been able to resist political pressures to eliminate discrimination in favor of foreign firms. And even while discrimination remains, politically influential domestic firms often succeed in obtaining foreign identity, in order to capture the special benefits available to foreigners. Moreover, refusals to extend tax holidays when they expire will lower redundancy rates. Many officials, however, have not been able to resist claims that the old investors cannot compete against new investors that have holidays. Strong stances on extensions will lower costs.

There are ways to reduce the costs of tax holidays, probably without lowering their impact, even if redundancy rates cannot be attacked. The influence of tax holidays may come primarily from their marketing impact, because they signal a welcoming attitude by the host government, rather than for the higher after-tax profits they yield. It is possible that this effect is especially significant in a period immediately after a country adjusts from hostile policies to investor-friendly policies. Officials of small countries sometimes also maintain that advertising incentives is simply the only way they can attract the attention of investors.

Another reason that incentives have an impact apart from the way they affect profits derives from bureaucratic behavior inside firms. Business negotiators insist on holidays and other incentives to show their superiors that they are good bargainers.[95] If these kinds of marketing and bureaucratic reasons dominate in the positive effects of incentives, tax holidays can be designed to reduce their costs without greatly reducing their effectiveness. Carryforward of losses out of the tax holiday period can, for example, be limited or even abolished. The investor can be required to take accelerated depreciation from the time assets are put in place. The clock on tax holidays can start ticking when they are granted, regardless of when production starts. And so on.

Obviously, business managers are sharp enough to understand the effect of such changes that lower costs to the host country. Yet, if the impact of incentives is primarily as a signal of welcome and as "trophies" for negotiators, rather than their effect on after-tax profits, then these efforts at cost reduction probably do not substantially reduce the impact of incentives as marketing tools. A country can still advertise, say, five-year tax holidays to foreign investors, and negotiators can still report their successes to their bosses.

Arguments in favor of tax holidays are often based on comparisons with policies of neighboring countries.[96] Competitive use of tax holidays is especially likely to emerge in free-trade areas or common markets. Indeed, there is some evidence that tax holidays are especially likely to affect locations of projects within such regions.[97] It is probable, for example, that Ireland's incentives induced a number of firms to locate there, rather than elsewhere in Europe, to serve the single European market. There is, however, no evidence to suggest that tax holidays influence the *total* amount of investment going to a trade area, only its location within the region. Thus, member countries face a prisoners' dilemma.[98] They would all gain if they could agree to reduce tax incentives, since they would collect more taxes and investment would not fall significantly. Recognizing this, the European Union has from its inception limited incentives by its member countries. All national investment incentives, including tax holidays, have to be calculated as grant equivalents. The value of such grants is limited to a specified percentage of the total investment, with the percentage varying according to the level of development in the area attracting the investment.

There have been efforts in other regions to negotiate limits on incentives, as well. In ASEAN, several attempts to negotiate restraints have failed. In fact, the Asian economic crisis led to a perverse result:

in the 1998 summit of ASEAN, member countries agreed to offer a *minimum* three-year tax holiday (or a minimum 30 percent corporate investment tax allowance) to investors from inside or outside the region.[99] This agreement emerged in spite of internal reassessments of the value of tax incentives that were going on in Thailand and the Philippines because of budgetary problems. Even though ASEAN has failed over the years to limit incentives, other regional groups may gain by adding limits on incentives to their agendas.[100]

For a country that is not a member of a free-trade area that has created a real single market, there is a strong case for unilaterally reducing or eliminating tax incentives, regardless of the incentives offered by neighbors. Because eliminating tax incentives is unlikely to lead to significant reductions in investment, as Indonesia's experience indicates, eliminating the high costs that they impose on the country will usually represent a net gain even if neighbors maintain their incentives.

The continuing influence of comparisons with neighboring countries, even in the absence of a free-trade arrangement, makes a strong case for a global agreement that would limit incentives competition, but the failure of past efforts suggests that the prospects for global limits are not encouraging. The most effective antidotes are probably regional agreements to limit competition, even in the absence of effective free-trade arrangements.

Yet in the short run, one cannot even be optimistic about the conclusion of regional agreements. The persistence of tax holidays, in spite of the evidence that costs often exceed benefits, leads one to turn to other policies. The pressures in favor of tax incentives in Indonesia suggest additional ways to reduce unproductive incentives and thus help the treasuries of developing countries.

Demands for tax incentives often come from investment-promotion offices, whose positions are driven by agency problems and the hidden nature of the costs of incentives. As long as incentives may cause *some* increase in foreign investment, the investment office is likely to press for them. One can imagine a policy response that involves calculations of costs of incentives that are granted.[101] Although publishing these costs will help weaken the pressure for incentives, allocating them to the budget of the organization that is to attract investors may more directly affect support for incentives.

The temptation to increase incentives seems especially great in times of crisis. In 1972, at the height of the Vietnam War, Vietnam's finance minister asked one of the authors of this essay whether investors were staying away from the country because tax incentives were not extensive enough; he was considering granting longer tax holidays. Similarly, Indonesia's response to the Asian economic crisis was to move ahead with more incentives. Yet, when policies are hostile to investment or the environment is otherwise unattractive, it is not at all obvious that tax incentives can offset the problems. If investors fear that political uncertainty, civil disturbances, or war will lead to losses, to the inability of affiliates to be reliable suppliers, or to dangers for expatriate staff—as was the case in Vietnam in 1972 and Indonesia in 2000—no amount of tax holidays can provide adequate compensation. Tax holidays benefit only firms that are profitable, and they do nothing to offset disturbances to supply chains, risks to personnel, threats to corporate strategy, or conflicts with local partners. Similarly, tax holidays are unlikely to be attractive counterbalances for a burdensome bureaucracy or unwanted local ownership or other requirements imposed on foreign investors. They are probably unconvincing in providing compensation for high corporate tax rates, since the investor will recognize that the high rates will apply when the holidays have expired. Using incentives as "fixes" in such situations should be avoided. They are unlikely to work; moreover, the ease with which they can be enacted tends to postpone a country's implementation of the more difficult steps that may really attract investors.

In sum, tax holidays are very costly and not very effective. Support for them arises at least in part from agency problems, the fact that costs are largely hidden, constant comparisons with neighbors, and the comparative ease with which incentives can be enacted. But tax holidays seem to be neither necessary nor sufficient for a country to attract foreign direct investment. Unilateral, regional, or global efforts to limit them are likely to contribute substantially to development.

Appendix A
Sample Statistical Results

A number of sets of regressions were calculated. The investment figures for 1983 and 1984 were handled in two different ways, to reflect the uncertainty that results from the acceleration of applications and the predating of approvals. In one set of tests, the 1983 and 1984 figures were eliminated. In another, they were averaged. All tests were carried out both on the value of foreign investment approved and on the number of projects approved. All tests were run with and without the large refinery investments that were never implemented. Regardless of the assumptions, there was no statistically significant difference between the growth rates of foreign investment before and after the elimination of tax holidays. Some sample results follow.

Table 3. Summary Statistics, Number of Projects and 1983–84 Figures Averaged

Regression statistics

Multiple R	0.97
R square	0.93
Adjusted R sq.	0.92
Standard error	0.15
Observations	16.00

Analysis of variance	df	SS	MS	F	Significance F
Regression	3	3.91	1.30	56.61	0.00
Residual	12	0.28	0.02		
Total	15	4.19			

	Coef-ficient	Standard error	t statistic	P-value	Lower 95%	Upper 95%
Intercept	1.57	0.14	11.14	0.00	1.27	1.88
After 1984	0.11	0.17	0.63	0.54	−0.26	0.47
1984	0.06	0.04	1.65	0.13	−0.02	0.14
Interaction	0.06	0.04	1.47	0.17	−0.03	0.15

Table 4. Summary Statistics, Number of Projects and 1983–84 Figures Omitted

Regression statistics

Multiple R	0.97
R square	0.94
Adjusted R sq.	0.92
Standard error	0.16
Observations	14.00

Analysis of variance	df	SS	MS	F	Significance F
Regression	3.00	3.65	1.22	49.74	0.00
Residual	10.00	0.24	0.02		
Total	13.00	3.90			

	Coef-ficient	Standard error	t statistic	P-value	Lower 95%	Upper 95%
Intercept	1.54	0.21	7.34	0.00	1.07	2.01
After 1984	0.21	0.24	0.89	0.39	−0.32	0.74
1984	0.05	0.05	1.06	0.31	−0.06	0.16
Interaction	0.05	0.05	1.01	0.34	−0.06	0.17

Appendix B
Sample Calculations of Subsidy Equivalents

The table should be read as follows: if projects have a 20 percent return on assets and if the redundancy rate for tax holidays is 70 percent, then the tax holidays are equivalent to a subsidy of 51 percent of the value of incremental investment attracted.

Table 5. Subsidy Equivalents, Using a 5-Year Tax Holiday, 10% Discount Rate, and 35% Tax Rate

Redundancy rate (in percent)	Rate of return on assets (in percent)			
	10	15	20	25
20	3	4	5	7
30	5	7	9	12
40	7	11	14	18
50	11	16	22	27
60	16	24	33	41
70	25	38	51	63
80	43	65	87	109
90	98	147	196	244

Table 6. Subsidy Equivalents, Using a 10-Year Tax Holiday, 10% Discount Rate, and 35% Tax Rate

Redundancy rate (in percent)	Rate of return on assets (in percent)			
	10	15	20	25
20	3	5	7	8
30	6	9	12	14
40	9	13	18	22
50	13	20	27	34
60	20	30	40	51
70	31	47	63	79
80	54	81	108	135
90	121	182	243	304

Table 7. Subsidy Equivalents, Using a 5-Year Tax Holiday, 10% Discount Rate, and 45% Tax Rate

Redundancy rate (in percent)	Rate of return on assets (in percent)			
	10	15	20	25
20	3	5	7	9
30	6	9	12	15
40	9	14	19	23
50	14	21	28	35
60	21	31	42	52
70	33	49	65	81
80	56	84	112	140
90	126	189	251	314

Notes

1. Tax incentives have a long history. The earliest tax incentives we have identified appeared in 1160, when wool weavers were offered tax incentives to locate in Biella, in the Piedmont region of northern Italy. This was apparently reported in Castronovo (1996, pp. 32–37). We have not seen this source; the reference comes from a manuscript sent to Wells with the manuscript author's name removed; we apologize to the manuscript author for not being able to give him or her proper credit for this interesting bit of history. Another early modern example of tax incentives comes from the then-"developing" part of the United States—Greene County, Georgia—in 1899. The offer was to exempt all manufacturing from taxes (presumably, property taxes), in an effort to encourage the relocation of textile mills from the more industrialized Northeast. The incentives were part of a promotion effort, which included a pamphlet issued in the same year by the "Development Company" to point out the great advantages to a manufacturer of location in the Georgia community. This example is cited in Raper (1943, p. 174).

2. The legislation added other incentives, such as guarantees against expropriation, guarantees on remittances abroad, exemptions from duties on capital equipment, and exemption from duties on raw materials for two years. Officials also believed that Indonesia had, in 1967, more liberal policies on domestic ownership requirements than did other countries in the

region. On the other hand, foreign firms were not allowed to borrow rupiah from local banks. This information was gained from interviews with Professor Mohammad Sadli in June 2000 and from Sadli (1995, pp. 35–51).

3. Law 1 of 1967.

4. The law contained an additional exemption for reinvested profits. In June 2000 interviews, Professor Sadli interpreted this as applying mainly to corporate tax on profits of firms that did not have a holiday. Wells, however, recalls that at the time there was some debate as to whether earnings from reinvested profits were to be exempted from corporate tax. We have found no clarifying documentation on this issue. The law specifies no time limit on this provision.

5. Under Law 6 of 1968.

6. Professor Sadli argued that "if foreign investors were given numerous rights, then ethically, economically, and politically the same rights should be given to domestic investors," in BKPM (n.d., p. 106).

7. From interviews with Professor Sadli in June 2000. In fact, elsewhere there has been a fear that offering incentives to foreigners without offering the equivalent to domestic investors would lead to "round-tripping," whereby domestic capital would be exported and reimported with a foreign label, as has happened with China. In fact, this problem materialized later in Indonesia, as foreign borrowing was treated differently for foreign and domestic firms. Humpuss Liberia, for example, applied for and received a foreign investment license for a chemical plant in Indonesia, even though the Humpuss Group was widely known to be Indonesian owned. Alternatively, domestic firms may seek silent foreign partners to obtain favorable classifications for their projects.

8. BKPM, "Sejarah Perkembangan Penanaman Modal," Draft III.2, apparently the final version, undated (early 1990s) and interviews with Professor Sadli in June 2000.

9. Law 11 of 1970 concerning Amendment and Supplement to Law 1 of 1967 Concerning Foreign Investment.

10. Jeffrey Winters claims that the exemption from dividend withholding tax applied only if the investor's home country did not tax the income. We have found no evidence to support this exception. The basic laws make no distinction by source of investment, but practice may have done so.

Such a "soak-up tax," as it is known, would have threatened foreign tax credits in the United States for any dividend taxes paid in Indonesia. See Winters (1996, p. 169, footnote 69), and see note 9 for Law 11 of 1970, "Dividend Tax."

11. Based on Wells's experience as an adviser to the investment agency in 1968–71 and interviews with Professor Sadli in June 2000. Although incentives were granted rather automatically, foreign investors had to obtain approvals for their projects, and all investments that went through the BKPM were subject to capacity licensing. Obtaining approval could be a long, drawn-out process and required the president's signature. Opponents could mobilize pressures against approval, arguing, for example, that sufficient capacity had already been approved for the particular industry.

12. See, in particular, Government Regulation No. 2 of 1981, for example (described in BKPM n.d., p. 38).

13. References to tax rates are all to the highest marginal rate.

14. The tax reform is carefully described by the lead Harvard adviser, Malcolm Gillis (1985, pp. 221–254).

15. The results of this study are reported by the Harvard Institute for International Development (HIID), "Impact of Tax Reform on Foreign Investors," September 15, 1983, in Buehrer (2000). "The results show that the incentive of a low (35 percent) tax rate has almost exactly the same impact on investors' returns as the old tax rates (of up to 45 percent) combined with the tax holidays." The memorandum went on to report the internal rate of return in 31 projects under the two tax regimes, using projections submitted by investors to the BKPM. HIID served as advisers to the ministry of finance during the design and implementation of the tax reform. The study is referred to in Gillis (1985, p. 248).

16. For the importance of these studies, see statements of Dono Iskandar, quoted in footnote 70 of Winters (1996, p. 170) and references to other officials (Winters 1996, pp. 171–172).

17. See HIID, "Tax Holidays and Direct Foreign Investment: Policy Issues," September 5, 1983, in Buehrer (2000). See also Gillis (1985, p. 247).

18. An HIID memorandum described tax holidays as having a bias in favor of capital intensity and against small-scale firms and projects. See note 17 for "Tax Holidays and Direct Foreign Investment" and Buehrer (2000).

19. The use of tax holidays had expanded from their original use for encouraging investment to include incentives for "going public." In contrast to analyses of tax incentives for investment, the tax incentives that were to encourage firms to issue stock on the new stock exchange were subjected to cost-benefit analyses. It was shown in one case that the costs to the treasury of the foregone taxes amounted to more than twice the value of the shares the company issued on the stock exchange. These calculations were made by Wells as a part of HIID's advisory work on tax reform. This incentive and other "bizarre" incentives are found in Gillis (1985, p. 245).

20. The incentives for issuing shares on the stock exchange became a frequently cited example.

21. Pages subsequent to 173 describe more reactions in Jakarta.

22. Quoted in BKPM (n.d., p. 108). See also Winters (1996, p. 178).

23. Cited in Winters (1996, pp. 177–178).

24. See, for example, statements of J.B. Sumarlin, chairman of BAPPENAS, cited in Winters (1996, p. 175).

25. No reliable and independent figures are available for realized investment. Those in the balance of payments are calculated by formula from approvals numbers.

26. Data for foreign investment approvals in Indonesia do not conform to international norms for measuring foreign direct investment, since they report the total value of projects with foreign equity, not simply the amount of foreign equity and parent loans. Because we are interested in changes, the reported data are, however, adequate. Implementation figures would be preferable to approvals, but they are quite unreliable for Indonesia; in fact, they have usually been calculated by formulas from approval figures. Not surprisingly, available data on implemented investments showed patterns similar to those of approvals. For 1983, investment showed an abnormal increase, of about 34 percent compared with 1980–81. And 1984 numbers showed a 20 percent decline on the same base. But the 1984 figures were 10 percent above those of the base years; by 1985–86, the increase was about 37 percent. That is, investment slowed and then grew again, and more rapidly than in the past. Source: HIID, "Interesting Trends in Foreign and Domestic Investment: A Summary," July 22, 1988 (in Buehrer 2000).

27. Obviously, the average size of a project before 1984 was larger than that after 1984. The averages were influenced by large mining and industrial projects in the earlier period; the later period saw increased inflows of investment (especially from other East Asian countries) for smaller projects for export manufacture.

28. See HIID, "Interesting Trends in Foreign and Domestic Investment: A Summary," July 22, 1988, in Buehrer (2000). This memorandum reported: "Abolition of tax holidays under the 1983 tax reform had, at most, very slight, temporary effects on the growth of foreign and domestic investment. The main effect was to induce a large rescheduling of proposals from later years forward to 1983 to enable firms to take advantage of the double incentive of pre-tax-reform tax holidays and post-tax-reform reduced tax rates. Most of this rescheduling was in the manufacturing sector." The memo attributed the especially strong investment performance of 1987 to the reform package of May 6, 1986.

29. James R. Hines, Jr. (1998) claims that tax sparing provisions in tax treaties lead to more investment. The claim is based on a demonstration that the ratio of Japanese investment to American investment is higher in countries that have tax sparing treaties with Japan than in countries that do not. The findings are, however, consistent with an alternative hypothesis that we find more plausible: that the Japanese negotiate tax treaties with countries where Japanese firms are most likely to go anyway. The countries with such treaties with Japan tend to be in Southeast and East Asia, Japan's backyard. Such treaties are much scarcer in Latin America, far from Japan and where American investors tend to go anyway. Nor surprisingly, the United Kingdom has negotiated similar treaties where its investors tend to go: former British colonies and former zones of influence, such as Cyprus. Our experience is that a critical mass of investors generates pressures for their home country to negotiate tax treaties with countries where they locate, rather than the opposite. Note also that Japanese investors and institutions led the early unsuccessful efforts to restore tax holidays in Indonesia (see pp. 27–31). Most field studies have focused on U.S. firms, but the theoretical impact of different home country tax systems is explored in Shah (1995, pp. 15–16, 30).

30. For analytical purposes, these nationalities are separated because the authors are somewhat uncertain as to the actual practice with respect to foreign-earned income in these countries.

31. Figures for 1985 were used for the breakpoint, rather than for 1984, since they were readily available.

32. As indicated later, during the years after tax holidays were eliminated, Indonesia made a number of policy changes. The need to continue to attract foreign investment added to pressures for reforms, which contributed to the country's rapid growth rate.

33. For an analysis of the impact of rather similar policies in Mexico on the inflow of foreign direct investment, see Graham and Wada (2000).

34. In fact, foreign direct investment flows to Hong Kong were even larger than flows to India, which had by this time turned more hospitable to foreign investment than in the past.

35. The flows can be compared easily from the data in annex table 1 of UNCTAD (1999).

36. For estimates of 20–25 percent, see Huang (1998) and World Bank (1996).

37. The amount of investment entering Hong Kong and then being moved on to other Asian countries is terribly difficult to estimate. Reported figures for stocks of FDI in Hong Kong are presumably measures of investment actually staying in Hong Kong. Those figures are very large on a per capita basis (almost $170 billion at the end of 1997). The total reported is close to 10 times the amount of foreign investment Hong Kong claims outside China. See tables 7 and 11 of U.S. Department of State (1999).

38. There are a number of summaries of the literature on tax incentives. Two excellent and recent surveys are Morisset and Pirnia (in this volume) and Oman (2000).

39. Several of the studies reported in Shah (1995) fall into this category. The editor discusses this approach to research on page 17. For actual efforts, see as examples chapters 1, 2, and 3, which report on research by Robin Boadway, Anwar Shah, Alan Auerbach, and Jack Mintz.

40. For two carefully done and early studies of such strategies, see Graham (1974) and Knickerbocker (1973).

41. See examples with regard to financial issues in Robbins and Stobaugh (1973).

42. Others have not found tax rates to be significant in explaining investment flows. See, for example, Lipsey (2000, p. 5).

43. Moreover, if aggregate government data are used for econometric work on the impact of incentives, the work is plagued by problems of colinearity. Incentives are usually associated with other favorable policies toward foreign investment. One cannot tell which led to the investment.

44. Chapter IV of UNCTAD (1996) summarizes and cites the following research: E. R. Barlow and I. T. Wender, *Foreign Investment and Taxation* (Englewood Cliffs: Prentice Hall, 1955); J. N. Behrman, "Foreign Associates and Their Financing," in Raymond F. Mikesell (ed.), *United States Private and Government Investment Abroad* (Eugene, Ore.: University of Oregon Press, 1962); R. S. Basi, *Determinants of United States Private Direct Investments in Foreign Countries* (Kent, Ohio: Kent State University, 1964); E. Kolde, *International Business Enterprise* (London: Prentice Hall, 1968); J. F. Chow, *Taxation and Multinational Enterprise* (London: Longman, 1974); D. J. C. Forsyth, *U.S. Investments in Scotland* (New York: Praeger, 1972); S. N. Acharya, "Incentives for Resource Allocation: A Case Study of Sudan," World Bank Working Paper 367 (Washington, D.C., 1979); O. Agodo, "The Determinants of U.S. Private Manufacturing Investments in Africa," *Journal of International Business Studies*, Vol. 9, 1978, pp. 95–107; W. D. Ingram and S. R. Pearson, "The Impact of Investment Concessions on the Profitability of Selected Firms in Ghana," *Economic Development and Cultural Change*, Vol. 29, 1981, pp. 831–839; P. O'Sullivan, "Determinants and Impact of Private Foreign Investment in Host Countries," *Management International Review*, Vol. 25, 1985, pp. 28–42; J. Weiss, "Alliance for Production: Mexico's Incentives for Private Sectoral Industrial Development," *World Development*, Vol. 12, pp. 723–742; R. Antoine, *Tax Incentives for Private Investment in Developing Countries* (Boston: Kluwer, 1979); A. Shah and J. F. Toye, "Fiscal Incentives for Firms in Some Developing Countries: Survey and Critique," in J. F. Toye (ed.), *Taxation and Economic Development* (London: Frank Cass, 1978); Group of Thirty, *Foreign Direct Investment: 1973–87* (New York: Group of Thirty, 1992); Guisinger and associates (1985).

45. See, particularly, Guisinger and associates (1985) and the summary of that research in Wells (1986). Nevertheless, Indonesia's incremental tax holidays for investment outside Java seem to have had little impact on

investment in the more remote areas. Under the old tax holiday scheme, 79 percent of foreign investment went to Java and Sumatra; during the entire 1967 to 1995 period, 77 percent. Under tax holidays, 4 percent went to Eastern Indonesia; over the 1967 to 1995 period, 6 percent. These figures are calculated from table 3.5 of Hill (1988), and use 1985 as the breakpoint. Eastern Indonesia includes Bali, Nusa Tenggara, Maluku, and Irian Jaya. In the four years before the tax holidays were dropped, Java received 64.7 percent of foreign investments; in the next two four-year periods, 64.4 percent and 64.1 percent. See BKPM (n.d., table 4, p. 84).

46. Oman (2000) argues that incentives affect decisions primarily in automobile manufacture and a few other industries with especially large investments.

47. Our view is that incentives matter especially little when the host country's general income tax rate is below some threshold level, perhaps 25–30 percent. But we are not aware of an empirical study that carefully examines this hypothesis.

48. Research on this issue could have a significant impact on the design of incentives (see Conclusions). Spar (1998) points out that the incentives and attention from the Costa Rican government increased Intel's feeling of security that the government would help if it needed it. Soehoed referred to tax holidays as "sales gimmicks" . . . that are more important in selling projects to stockholders than for increasing returns (Winters 1996, p. 178). In discussions of incentives, Raymond Vernon (who was head of the Multinational Enterprise Project at the Harvard Business School in the 1960s and 1970s) often hypothesized that their impact came largely from the signals they gave that foreign investors were welcome in the country. A different concept of tax holidays as a marketing device appears in Bond and Samuelson (1986). They argue that tax holidays can be used to deal with asymmetric information, where the country knows more about costs than the investor. The Bond-Samuelson argument would be more convincing for incentives other than tax holidays. An investor who is uncertain as to whether high costs will mean no profits is much more likely to be influenced by incentives that directly reduce costs, as opposed to tax holidays, which benefit the investor only if profits materialize.

49. See exceptions in Oman (2000), who suggests figures like $100,000 per job created. Another important effort to calculate costs as well as benefits is in Robert Halvorsen, "Fiscal Incentives for Investment in Thailand," in Shah (1995).

50. *But for* has become a term of art in evaluating incentives in the United States. See later reference to Hinkley and others (2000). Note that the government's cost of subsidies to attract an incremental firm differs from the subsidy actually received by that firm, since the government's cost includes awards to firms that would have come anyway.

51. One could also discount the subsidies granted each year to arrive at a net present value. Here, the calculations are kept simple, since the estimates of redundancy rates are crude.

52. Calculating the benefits of any incremental foreign investment attracted by incentives requires an assessment of shadow prices and externalities. This is beyond the scope of this paper. It is doubtful, however, that calculations for any of today's relatively open economies would justify very high subsidy equivalents.

53. Fiscal Policy Office, Fiscal and Tax Policy Division, Ministry of Finance, "Study on Fiscal Implications of Investment Incentives and Promotion Efficiency," report prepared by Industrial Management Co., Ltd., in association with IMG Consultants Pty., Ltd., Bangkok, and reported in Robert Halvorsen, "Fiscal Incentives for Investment in Thailand," in Shah (1995).

54. One could argue that the redundancy rates for foreign and domestic firms are not quite comparable. An increase in profits of foreign firms is likely to result in a real cost to the economy, while larger profits of a domestic firm represent only a transfer within the country.

55. It seems that Indonesians understood the cost of extensions. Sumarlin, when he was minister of finance, made it clear to parliament that an approach used in Indonesia—simply starting a new enterprise to obtain new tax holidays when the old ones expire—meant a loss of revenue (see Winters 1996, p. 181).

56. The possibility of such "tax arbitrage" is recognized in Shah (1995, p. 8) and in considerable detail in Galper and Walton (1999).

57. Lest the reader conclude that it was only these reforms that meant the continuation of growth for foreign investment after incentives were eliminated, note that foreign investment had recovered in 1985 and 1986, before the reforms had really begun.

58. For evidence of the spread from the mid-1980s to the early 1990s, see UNCTAD (1996, table III.1, p. 19).

59. The Harvard group continued to advise the ministry of finance and the economic coordinating minister during the 1980s and 1990s.

60. "Comments on Oshima's 'Indonesia Investment Climate: Opportunities for Japanese Investors,'" August 21, 1986 (in Buehrer 2000).

61. "Coopers and Lybrand Draft Report," August 8, 1986.

62. "Preparation of a New Trade Policy Package: Effects on Foreign Investment in Indonesia," May 5, 1987 (in Buehrer 2000).

63. Prepared by the SGV Group, an accounting firm.

64. "Consequences of Income Tax Holidays and Tax Incentives," November 28, 1991 (in Buehrer 2000).

65. "Additional Tax Holidays for Special Projects," May 25, 1993; and "Tax Holidays," May 22, 1993 (in Buehrer, 2000).

66. "Memoranda on Tax Holidays and Deregulation," April 18, 1996 (comprising four earlier memos, in Buehrer 2000).

67. This, of course, is in addition to any income that might accrue to individuals within the organization for their powers to grant or withhold value.

68. Walter P. Falcon (Stanford University) has stated the phenomenon as follows: "One good story is worth a thousand research studies." This seems to hold whether or not the one story is typical.

69. It should be noted that the electronics firms attracted to Indonesia in the early 1970s had come under tax holidays. Some managers believe that they left because of the continuing difficulty of business in Indonesia, especially in getting imported components delivered quickly and free of unofficial payments; others argued that the firms left because of problems at home. In any event, tax holidays were not the issue.

70. The impact on advisers is illustrated in a 1996 memo by Jeffrey Sachs, then head of the Harvard Institute for International Development, to the coordinator of HIID projects in Indonesia, in support of tax holi-

days, which staff in the field had long opposed. In the memo, Sachs ordered: "I want to have a thorough review of the evidence on tax holidays. . ." and a study of their effectiveness. His insistence—"I would like this issue looked into closely"—seemed not to recognize the large volume of research already done on the subject or Indonesia's own experience, and it did not indicate any need to examine the cost side. The order was based on a single conversation with the managing director of the Malaysian subsidiary of a U.S. firm. That firm was, in fact, widely known to insist on incentives (preferably subsidies) and was indeed the same firm that had earlier tried to get offers from Indonesia to increase its bargaining power elsewhere in the region (see pp. 30–31). Source: "Location Decisions for Malaysian Firms [sic]," from e-mail files of the HIID project in Indonesia, September 25, 1996. Sachs has frequently used the same story to argue for tax incentives elsewhere.

71. Although the elimination of tax incentives in 1984 did occur under an atmosphere that might be called experimental, in fact the 1996 changes occurred under a rather different climate. Still, the nature of the change provides something like a natural experiment for testing the impact.

72. Government Regulation No. 34/1994, dated November 16, 1994, "Taxation Facilities for Capital Investments in Certain Business Fields and/or Certain Areas," translation in *Business News*, December 12, 1994. For the application, see "Tax as a Policy Instrument," *Business News*, December 2, 1994.

73. Presidential Decree No. 75/1994, dated November 16, 1994, "Income Tax Facilities for Esso Exploration and Production Natuna Inc. Drilling and Processing Natural Gas on Natuna Islands and Nearby Sea on a Profit Sharing Contract." The language is not perfectly clear on the withholding tax.

74. Government Regulation No. 45/1996, dated July 8, 1996.

75. Some Indonesian officials deny that this decree called for tax holidays. The wording of the decree says that the government will pay the corporate income tax on behalf of the investor. The effect, of course, is the same as a tax holiday. Other incentives that crept into the system in 1996 and soon thereafter are documented in Galper and Walton (1999). These authors describe the move as going down a "slippery slope."

76. This list reflects an amendment to the original decree, Presidential Decree No. 61/1996, dated August 12, 1996.

77. In the United States, this has been labeled the *but for* rule. See Hinkley and others (2000).

78. Interview held in Jakarta in June 2000.

79. Presidential Decree No. 38/1997, dated September 1, 1997, "The Granting of Tax Facilities to Certain Industries," translation in *Business News*, September 3, 1997. Various sources report the number of recipients of incentives at 6, 9, and 18; in fact, the numbers 6 and 9 appear in the same article. Apparently in 1997 there were 13 more applications pending, but there is no evidence that more companies actually received tax holidays. See Industry (1997) and Castle Group, *Indonesian Business: The Year in Review*, 1998, chapter 2, http://www.castleasia.com/products/yir/1998/ch2.html. See also: Jose Manuel Tesoro, "Past vs. Future: The Texmaco Scandal Is a Test Case—One in Which Indonesian Business Confronts Suharto's Legacy," *Asia Week.com*, December 24, 1999, Vol. 25, No. 51 (http://www.cnn.com/ASIANOW/asiaweek/magazine/99/1224/biz.indonesia.texmaco.html).

80. See note 79, Tesoro.

81. See, for example, "Some Ear Biting Players," *Gatra*, Number 4/VI, December 11, 1999.

82. Listed in Hamzah Haz, "9 Tax Holiday Dikaji Ulang," *Bisnis Indonesia*, June 8, 1998.

83. One could debate whether the smelter was pioneer. Freeport already mined copper in Indonesia, and its contract of work may have contained a commitment for a smelter.

84. Interviewed for this research in June 2000.

85. It is not even clear that tax holidays were necessary to attract the two pioneer foreign firms.

86. See note 82.

87. See also Jeffrey Krasner, "Tax Credits May Violate Vt. Policy," *The Wall Street Journal*, September 20, 2000, p. NE1.

88. In an extreme example of tax incentives that were poorly designed to attract hesitant investors, in 2000 decisions about some of the incentives that officials in Nigeria could award were not made until after the investor had made really substantial commitments to a project.

89. Presidential Decree No. 89/1996, dated December 3, 1996, "Integrated Economic Development Zones."

90. "Use of Fiscal Incentives,"September 2, 1999 (in Buehrer 2000).

91. "Government Mulling Incentives to Lure Back Foreign Investors," *Jakarta Post*, May 24, 2000.

92. "Editorial II: Can Investments be Stimulated with More Fiscal Incentives?" *Business News*, May 31, 2000.

93. Third Amendment to Law 7 of 1983, according to "Maximum Investment Allowance 30%," *Business News*, June 7, 2000.

94. Although reliable figures are not available, it seems that a large portion of the post-1986 investment from Korea and Taiwan, in particular, was for export. It appears that Thailand got a proportionally large share of Taiwan export investment and Indonesia, of Korean investment. The allocation is often explained by the belief that Chinese investors felt more comfortable in the more-integrated Thailand.

95. This explanation of managers' behavior was often offered by Raymond Vernon in discussions of bargaining between business managers and government officials. Wells remembers his having proposed this explanation as early as 1968, when he was confronted with what seemed to be irrational behavior by U.S. managers who were insisting on tax incentives even in cases in which most resulting gains would clearly be offset by increased tax payments in the firms' home country.

96. The Southeast Asian competition, as one country copies tax incentives introduced by neighbors, is described in Galper and Walton (1999). The pattern is also described in Negee Choon Chia and John Whalley, "Patterns in Investment Incentives among Developing Countries," in Shah (1995).

97. In the period studied, Indonesia was not part of an effective trade area.

98. Oman (2000) refers to the broader competition among countries for foreign investment as having the characteristics of a prisoners' dilemma. Graham (1966, appendix B; 2000) does so explicitly in the context of investment incentives. The concept has been at least implicit in a number of proposals, by C. Fred Bergsten (director of the Institute for International Economics) and others, for international agreements on foreign direct investment over the years.

99. *http://www.mida.gov.my/Aseanwn/Aseanwn.html.* In 2000, Indonesia apparently fulfilled its commitment under this provision with the 30 percent

investment allowance authorized as a replacement for the defunct 1996 tax holidays. See *Business News*, June 7, 2000, p. 4.

100. The case for regional or global limits on incentives has been made especially eloquently on several occasions by Edward M. Graham (2000). There were pressures at least as early as 1981 to include limits on investment incentives in what became the Uruguay Round. In the end, however, the agreement limited only incentives that were contingent on export performance. For brief histories of this and other international efforts to limit incentives, see Graham (1966, especially pp. 71–73).

101. The Irish Industrial Development Agency, for example, publishes the costs of some incentives it grants.

References

BKPM. n.d. *25 Years of Investment: A Brief History of Investment Development in Indonesia*. Jakarta: Ministry of Investment/Investment Coordinating Board.

Bond, E. W., and L. Samuelson. 1986. "Tax Holidays as Signals." *The American Economic Review* 76(4): 820–26.

Buehrer, Timothy, ed. 2000. "HIID CEM/EAP Memoranda and Interviews: 1985–2000." Harvard Institute for International Development, Jakarta, June, CD ROM.

Castronovo, V. 1996. "Biella: History Runs a Woolen Thread." *Arrivederci* VII (75): 32–37.

Galper, Harvey, and Geoffrey Walton. 1999. "Investment Tax Incentives: Recent Indonesian Experience and Options for Reform." USAID (U.S. Agency for International Development) Working Paper. Jakarta.

Gillis, Malcolm. 1985. "Micro and Macroeconomics of Tax Reform: Indonesia." *Journal of Development Economics* 19(3): 221–54.

Graham, Edward M. 1966. *Global Corporations and National Governments*. Washington, D.C.: Institute for International Economics.

———. 1974. "Oligopolistic Imitation and European Direct Investment in the United States." Ph.D. diss. Harvard University, Business School, Boston, Mass.

————. 2000. *Fighting the Wrong Enemy: Antiglobal Activists and Multinational Enterprises.* Washington, D.C.: Institute for International Economics.

Graham, Edward M., and Erika Wada. 2000. "Domestic Reform, Trade and Investment Liberalisation, Financial Crisis, and Foreign Direct Investment into Mexico." *The World Economy* 23(6): 777–97.

Guisinger, Steve, and associates. 1985. *Investment Incentives and Performance Requirements.* New York: Praeger.

Harink, Vincent G. 1984. "Do Recent Tax Changes Reduce Foreign Investment?" *East Asian Executive Reports* 6(8): 8.

Hill, Hal. 1988. *Foreign Investment and Industrialization in Indonesia.* Singapore: Oxford University Press.

Hines, James R., Jr. 1998. " 'Tax Sparing' and Direct Investment in Developing Countries." National Bureau of Economic Research Working Paper 6728. Cambridge, Mass.

————. 2000. "International Taxation," *NBER* (National Bureau of Economic Research) *Reporter*, Spring, p. 11.

Hinkley, Sara, Fiona Hsu, Greg LeRoy, and Katie Tallman. 2000. "Minding the Candy: State Audits of Economic Development," Good Jobs First (September), www.goodjobsfirst.org.

Huang, Yasheng. 1998. *F.D.I. in China: An Asian Perspective.* Singapore: Institute of Southeast Asian Studies.

"Industry: Government Provides Tax Holiday Incentive for Six Companies." 1997. PT Data Consult Inc./ Indonesia Commercial Newsletter, No. 228, 49–51.

Knickerbocker, F. T. 1973. *Oligopolistic Reaction and Multinational Enterprises.* Cambridge, Mass.: Harvard University, Business School.

Lipsey, Robert E. 2000. "Interpreting Developed Countries' Foreign Direct Investment." National Bureau of Economic Research Working Paper 7810. Cambridge, Mass.

Oman, Charles P. 2000. "Policy Competition for Foreign Direct Investment: A Study of Competition among Governments to Attract FDI." OECD Development Centre, Paris.

Raper, Arthur F. 1943. *Tenants of the Almighty.* New York: Macmillan.

Robbins, Sidney M., and Robert B. Stobaugh. 1973. *Money in the Multinational Enterprise: A Study of Financial Policy.* New York: Basic Books.

Sadli, Mohammad. 1995. "Recollections of My Career." *Bulletin of Indonesian Economic Studies* 29(1): 35–51.

Shah, Anwar, ed. 1995. *Fiscal Incentives for Investment and Innovation.* Oxford, Eng.: Oxford University Press.

Spar, Deborah. 1998. *Attracting High Technology Investment: Intel's Costa Rican Plant.* Foreign Investment Advisory Service Occasional Paper 11. Washington, D.C.

U.N. (United Nations). 1997. *World Investment Report 1997: Transnational Corporations, Market Structure and Competition Policy.* U.N. Transnational Corporations and Management Division, Department of Economic and Social Development. Geneva.

UNCTAD (United Nations Conference on Trade and Development). 1996. *Incentives and Foreign Direct Investment.* New York and Geneva: United Nations.

———. 1999. *Foreign Direct Investment and Development.* UNCTAD Series on Issues in International Investment Agreements. New York and Geneva: United Nations.

U.S. Department of State. 1999. *FY2000 Country Commercial Guide: Hong Kong.* Washington, D.C.: U.S. Government Printing Office.

Wells, Louis T., Jr. 1986. "Investment Incentives: An Unnecessary Debate." *The CTC Reporter* 22: 58–60.

Winters, Jeffrey A. 1996. *Power in Motion: Capital Mobility and the Indonesian State.* Ithaca and London: Cornell University Press.

World Bank. 1996. *Managing Capital Flows in East Asia.* Washington, D.C.: World Bank.

How Tax Policy
and Incentives Affect
Foreign Direct Investment

A Review

Jacques Morisset
Neda Pirnia

Acknowledgments

The Foreign Investment Advisory Service (FIAS) is a joint service of the International Finance Corporation and the World Bank. The opinions and arguments expressed are the sole responsibility of the authors and do not necessarily reflect those of these institutions.

We would like to thank Bijit Bora, Gokhan Akinci, and Carl Aaron for their comments.

Acronyms and Abbreviations

ASEAN	Association of Southeast Asian Nations
EPZ	Export processing zone
FDI	Foreign direct investment
OECD	Organisation for Economic Co-operation and Development
R and D	Research and development

1
Introduction

In a world where an increasing number of governments compete aggressively to attract multinational companies, fiscal incentives have become a global phenomenon. Poor African countries rely on tax holidays and import duty exemptions, while industrial Western European countries permit investment allowances or accelerated depreciation (see table on p. 72). This trend seems to have grown considerably since the early 1990s, as evidenced by the number of high-profile foreign investments, such as Toyota in northern France and Mercedes-Benz A.G. in Alabama in the United States. These have generated considerable debate about whether governments have offered unreasonably large incentives to entice those firms to invest in their areas. Still, this debate about the effectiveness of tax incentives is hardly new and has accumulated a long history.[1]

The objective of this essay is to review the existing literature on tax policy and foreign direct investment (FDI), as well as to explore possibilities for future research. Taxes affect the net return on capital and should, at least in the minds of numerous policymakers, influence the capital movements between countries. For this reason, the early literature attempted to evaluate whether a generous tax policy could compensate for other obstacles in the business environment and thus attract multinational companies. In the mid-

Types of Incentives Used, by Region

			Region				
			Latin America and	Central and Eastern	Western	Other	
Major incentives	Africa (23)	Asia (17)	Caribbean (12)	Europe (25)	Europe (20)	countries (6)	Total (103)
Tax holidays	16	13	8	19	7	4	67
Accelerated depreciation	12	8	6	6	10	5	47
Investment allowances	4	5	9	3	5		26
Import duty exemption	15	13	11	13	7	4	63
Duty drawback	10	8	10	12	6	3	49

Note: The number of countries in each region is in parentheses.
Source: UNCTAD 1995.

1980s, the literature went one step further by exploring what kinds of tax instruments should have the greatest impact on the location decisions of multinational companies. Special attention was also given to the motivations and tax behavior of multinational companies.

In recent years, the globalization process has led to the emergence of new issues. First, companies have tended to become more mobile, and governments have had to deal with this in the design of their national tax policies. The gradual elimination of barriers to capital movements has stimulated governments to compete for FDI in global markets and has reinforced the role of tax policy in this process. The recent competitive trend has to be offset by the increasing pressure that governments face to harmonize their tax policies within regional (or international) agreements. A second important issue is the recognition that tax policies of the home and host countries are interconnected and that this link influences the behavior of multinationals. There is a great deal of evidence, especially after the changes in the U.S. tax laws during the late 1980s, that home country tax policy affects both the multinational firm's behavior and the effectiveness of tax policies in the countries where the firm operates and invests. Last, but not least, there has been growing attention to the costs associated with tax incentives—and not only to their possible benefits. Tax incentives are likely not only to have a direct negative impact on fiscal revenues but also, and frequently, to create significant possibilities for suspicious behaviors from tax administrations and companies. This issue has become crucial in developing countries, where budgetary constraints and corruption are certainly more severe than in industrial countries.

This essay proceeds as follows: chapter 2 reviews the early literature that examines the impact of tax policy on FDI from a global perspective using investors' surveys and time-series econometric analysis. Chapter 3 explores which tax instruments have the greatest impact on FDI and what kinds of foreign investors are likely to be most responsive to changes in tax policy, since these two areas have retained the attention of many researchers over the past 15 years. Chapter 4 focuses on three issues that have emerged with globalization: the interconnection between the home and host countries' taxation and its subsequent impact on FDI; tax competition versus harmonization across countries and states; and the costs associated with tax incentive schemes. Chapter 5 concludes with a few remarks and ideas for future research.

2

Early Literature: The Aggregate Approach

Tax policies are obviously capable of affecting the volume and location of FDI, since all other considerations being equal, higher tax rates reduce after-tax returns. Of course, all other considerations are seldom equal. Countries not only differ in their tax policies but also in their commercial and regulatory policies, market size, natural endowments, and human capital. All these factors influence the desirability of an investment location.

Based on this perception, the early research attempts to determine if tax policy was one of the key factors in the decisionmaking process of multinational companies. Two basic approaches were, and continue to be, developed: (1) selective surveys of international investors and (2) time-series econometric analyses. The majority of earlier studies focus on the aggregate FDI data by lumping together firms of all types, and pay little attention to differences across sectors and industries, as well as between regions and countries. A brief summary of the major findings follows.

Survey of Investors

One of the first survey studies was conducted by Barlow and Wender in 1955. They interviewed 247 U.S. companies on their strategies to invest abroad. One of the questions asked was about the conditions that were required before the companies would proceed with foreign investment. Only 10 percent of the companies listed favorable foreign taxes as a condition for FDI, while another 11 percent mentioned "host government encouragement to companies." Together, these inducements were ranked fourth after currency convertibility, guarantee against expropriation, and host country political stability.

These findings are confirmed by the survey of 205 companies conducted by Robinson in 1961. Perhaps the most important result of Robinson's survey is the considerable difference of opinion between the business community and government with regard to the major factors influencing decisions to invest. Tax concessions headed the list of government responses, while they were omitted from the list of private investor responses.

Next comes the result of field research conducted by Aharoni and published in 1966 on the way foreign investment decisions were made by U.S. manufacturing firms. The conclusions are that host government concessions do not bring about the decisions to invest. Income tax exemption is considered a very weak stimulant. Those investors who do consider it, do it only marginally. In the words of one of the investors in the survey: "Tax exemption is like a dessert; it is good to have, but it does not help very much if the meal is not there." It should be noted that in this case, as in the case of Robinson's interviews, host government officials interviewed in the field research believed income tax exemption to be a very powerful stimulus to FDI.

In a 1984 survey of 52 multinational companies, the Group of Thirty found that among 19 factors that were identified as influencing FDI flows, inducements offered by the host country rank seventh in importance for investment in developing countries and eighth in industrialized countries. In recent years, several investors' surveys explore the effectiveness of tax policies on FDI using alternative samples or asking more-detailed questions (for example, Ernst & Young 1994; *Fortune*/Deloitte Touche 1997; Japan External Trade Organization 1995). In general, these surveys confirm the conclusions summarized above: that if tax policy matters, then it is not the most influential factor in the site selection of multinationals.[2]

Econometric Analysis

The available econometric evidence on the effect of taxation used time-series estimation of the responsiveness of FDI to annual variations in tax rates. Most econometric studies tend to confirm the results of surveys: that investors are mostly influenced in their decisions by market and political factors and that tax policy appears to have little effect on the location of FDI.

A selective sample of studies concludes in that direction: Root and Ahmed (1978), Agodo (1978), Shah and Toye (1978), and Lim (1983). In 1978, Root and Ahmed performed an econometric study with data for 41 developing countries for the period 1966–70. They classified countries into three categories—unattractive, moderately attractive, and highly attractive—according to their average annual per capita inflow of FDI. Then 44 variables were chosen as potentially significant discriminators of the three country groups. Among the six policy-related discriminators were three related to tax levels. Of these, corporate tax rates proved to be an effective discriminator of the three defined country groups; however, tax incentives laws and liberality were not found to be effective discriminators. In the same year, Agodo (1978) analyzed a sample of 33 U.S. firms having 46 manufacturing investments in 20 African countries. Tax concessions were found to be insignificant as a determinant of FDI in simple and multiple regressions.

Much of the research of the period uses highly aggregate data, evaluating the correlation between annual changes in FDI flows and a series of factors, including movements in after-tax rates of return earned by foreign investments. The primary limitation of aggregate studies is that changes in FDI may be correlated with important omitted variables, such as trade and financial liberalization, as well as the elimination of barriers against FDI. Most countries embark on a reform process that includes simultaneous actions aimed at enhancing the development of private investment, including FDI promotion. As a result, it becomes very difficult to distinguish the effects of taxation from the effects of other variables that are, in turn, correlated with tax rates.

There is also the crucial issue of how to define tax policy changes and to measure the after-tax rate of return. Which taxes should be included in the regressions (corporate profit tax, trade taxes, domestic indirect taxes, and the like)? Should these taxes be integrated in one aggregate or several indicators? Several studies employ nominal tax rates, but they can be misleading for a variety of reasons. In particular, they do not capture the eventual tax rebates that are offered to specific investments or activities. Understanding the exact impact of tax policy on investment decisions has led to the development of the popular concept of effective tax rate, which is defined as the percentage reduction in the financial rate of return on an investment that is due to the fiscal system of the host country.[3] In principle, both the effective marginal and average tax rates[4] may be relevant in the strategic decisions made by firms. Locating production in an area with a low marginal rate should lead to a high optimal level of output, while the average rate will affect the profit level.[5] In a recent econometric study on the behavior of U.S. firms in the European Union, Devereux and Griffith (1998) show that the average effective tax rates seem to have a greater impact on the FDI location than the marginal tax rates.

Still, the general conclusion that emerges from the early econometric studies is that the effect of tax policy on FDI is rather limited, at least compared with other factors, such as political stability, the costs and availability of labor, and basic infrastructure. The importance of these other factors suggests that tax policy is a poor instrument to compensate for various negative factors in the investment climate of a country. Many countries, from South America to Sub-Saharan Africa, have offered investment incentives for businesses to locate in underdeveloped, more costly, and otherwise unattractive regions with little success in generating (sustainable) investment flows to those areas. These experiences strongly suggest that the fiscal investment incentives popular in developing countries have not been effective in making up for fundamental weaknesses in the investment climate.

3

New Evidence from the Mid-1980s: A Search for Details

The relatively little importance of tax policy does not mean that it does not exert any impact on FDI. Looking at foreign direct investment figures, it is certainly not a coincidence that FDI in tax haven countries in the Caribbean and South Pacific grew more than fivefold between 1985 and 1994, to over $200 billion. Ireland's tax policy has generally been recognized as a key factor in its success in attracting international investors over the past two decades. In fact, the simple position described in the preceding section was not completely accurate. It is not true that tax policy and incentives fail to attract investors; they do affect the decisions of *some* investors *some* of the time.

Even in the 1970s, there were researchers who started to look into more-detailed FDI data and came out with conclusions that make the results of previous studies more vulnerable to criticism. Forsyth, in his 1972 study, provides support for the view that inducements and incentives often may not play a key role in influencing the decision to undertake a particular foreign investment. However, once other factors provoke the decision to set up production facilities in a broad

81

area, then the more precise location decision may be strongly affected by inducements and incentives.

By the mid-1980s, understanding the exact role of incentives in attracting FDI became a new research agenda. One direction has been to explore the reaction of multinational companies to changes in tax policy when they differ in their activities, motivations, market structure, and/or financing. Others have searched to examine which tax instruments may have the greater effect on the behavior of international investors.

Tax Behavior of Multinational Companies

While most early studies examine the impact of taxes on the average foreign investor, there are many reasons to believe that this impact differs greatly depending on the characteristics of the multinational company. International investors often have at their disposal numerous alternative methods of structuring and financing their investments, arranging their transactions between related parties located in different countries, and returning profits to investors. These alternatives have important tax implications, and there is considerable anecdotal evidence that tax considerations strongly influence the choices that firms make.

One of the earlier findings in the literature is that the impact of tax rates on investment decisions is generally higher on export-oriented companies than on those seeking the domestic market or location-specific advantages. In surveys, such firms are those with managers that have responded more favorably to tax incentives (see Reuber 1973[6] and Guisinger and others 1985). This finding is not really surprising because export-oriented firms, such as garment manufacturers, are operating in highly competitive markets with very slim margins. Moreover, these firms are often highly mobile and more likely to compare taxes across alternative locations (Wells 1986). Hence, taxes can be an important part of their cost structure, and the firms can easily move to take advantage of more-favorable tax regimes.

The impact and the nature of incentive schemes may also differ as they apply to either new or existing companies. For example, Rolfe and others (1993), using a survey of managers of U.S. firms, show that start-up companies prefer incentives that reduce their initial expenses (equipment and material exemption), while expanding firms prefer tax incentives that target profit. He also reports that manufacturing industries prefer incentives related to depreciable assets because they use more fixed assets than do service industries.

In an interesting study, Coyne (1994) suggests that small investors are generally more responsive to tax incentives than are large investors. Taxes may play a more important role in the cost structure of small companies because they do not have the financial and human capacity to develop sophisticated tax avoidance strategies. Large multinational companies are also more likely to receive special tax treatments, whatever the tax laws applied by the host country. Oman (2000) reports some evidence that large firms, especially in the automobile sector, are more likely to negotiate secret advance agreements on how much they will pay in both industrial and developing countries.

There exist a few studies that estimate separate equations for FDI financed by retained earnings and FDI financed by external funds (equity plus debt) (Hartman 1985; Boskin and Gale 1987). They typically found that FDI financed by retained earnings is more strongly influenced by host country tax rates. However, they do not offer any clear explanation for this result. It is also possible that equity and debt financing are influenced by the tax policy in the home country, thereby reducing the impact of the host country's tax regimes (see chapter 4 for more explanations).

Finally, there is growing evidence that low taxes may be a key factor for firms that are operating not in one specific market but in multiple markets, such as Internet-related businesses, insurance companies, and banks. Establishing a subsidiary in a low-tax country gives them the opportunity to develop tax avoidance strategies. It is indeed difficult for any one country to claim the right to tax the holding company if its operations take place in multiple markets at the same time. Here is a typical example: when filing tax returns in a high-tax country, a multinational company claims that it has earned as little profit as possible. Instead, it tries to attribute as much profit as possible to its operations in low-tax countries by arranging "transactions" between its subsidiaries in the two countries, and setting the "transfer price" of those transactions so that it has the desired effect on profits. Multinationals can also adjust the timing of their dividend repatriations from foreign subsidiaries (see Hines and Hubbard 1990). In practice, such strategies may explain the success of tax haven countries in attracting subsidiaries of global companies and the cost to multinationals of economists and accountants to justify transfer prices that suit their tax needs. Still, very little is known about the magnitude of such international tax evasion and how much it affects tax revenues across countries (see, for some preliminary evidence, Grubert, Goodspeed, and Swensson 1993 or Globalization 2000).

Tax Instruments Used by Governments

Governments have several tax instruments that they can use to attempt to influence the effective tax rates and the location decisions of multinational companies.[7] The literature has traditionally focused on the instruments linked to the corporate income tax, such as tax holidays and tax allowances. Of course, these instruments are of no help to an unprofitable company; therefore, other forms of incentives have also been widely used around the world. Exemptions from customs duties or local indirect taxes (generally to targeted sectors) do exist in many countries, even though their use has been restricted in most international and bilateral trade treaties. Outright grants are used in many industrial countries but rarely in the developing world because of their upfront costs.

Following the existing literature, our focus is on the corporate income tax and the different options used by governments to relieve companies of their tax burdens. Governments with high corporate tax rates have a number of options to reduce them to more competitive levels. One is to give tax incentives to a selected group of firms. An alternative is to change the general fiscal system to lower the effective tax rate for all firms. There are many options between these two extremes, including the "stability premium," that have been offered to investors by such countries as Chile and Colombia. This premium gives an investor the option to purchase the right to maintain its corporate tax rate at a given level, even if the tax regime will be modified in the future. A short review of the major options is presented below, but at the outset, it is worth underscoring that there is certainly no clear-cut answer in favor of one or another alternative mechanism (see Mintz and Tsiopoulos 1992, for fuller details).

The first option is to generalize a low corporate tax rate on a broad base. Small economies—such as Hong Kong, Lebanon, and Mauritius—have typically retained this option. A low corporate tax rate is, in itself, an incentive. It allows investors to keep a larger portion of profits. Governments are also able to maintain corporate tax revenues because investors have limited tax-planning opportunities and the simplicity of the system makes for an advantageous investment climate. Investors look favorably on a country offering a low statutory tax rate, especially one well below the worldwide norm of 35–40 percent, since it signals that the government is interested in letting the market determine the most profitable investments without undue governmental influence. Although a broad-based low corporate tax rate is appealing, this approach has limitations. In particular, international linkages can undermine a country's efforts to make its tax system relatively neutral. In fact, a country with a corporate tax system greatly out of line with other countries may be better off having a less neutral system, to minimize distortions. It also has to be recognized that the sudden change to a low, generalized tax rate can reduce tax revenues during a transition period, even though the simplicity of the tax system may attract further investors and increase the tax base in the longer run and so compensate for the initial reduction.

For these reasons, many governments rely on tax-incentive schemes in their effort to lure foreign investors. This selective approach, in contrast to a generalized tax reduction, is attractive to many countries because it may minimize the initial effect on fiscal revenues and, in principle, should help to target specific industries or activities that will bring the greater benefits to the country. It can also be argued that incentives may have a signaling effect on the government's commitments to stimulate FDI, as they are generally easier to implement than is a general reform of the tax system (see Bond and Samuelson 1986).

One popular form of tax incentive consists of reducing the corporate income tax rate by providing tax holidays or temporary rebates. This form of incentive has been popular in developing countries where authorities have favored a discretionary approach. For example, several African investment codes have included tax holidays, with differentiated rebates and periods of abatement, depending on the government's objectives. The main benefit of tax holidays is that they provide large benefits as soon as the company begins earning income, and are thus more valuable than an incentive, such as a lower corporate tax rate, that accrues more slowly over a longer period of time. However, they primarily benefit short-term investments, which often are undertaken in so-called footloose industries characterized by companies that can quickly disappear from one jurisdiction to reappear in another. Tax holidays also tend to reward the founding of a company, rather than investment in existing companies, and to discriminate against investments that rely on long-lived depreciable capital. Last but not least, they can lead to a large erosion of the tax base as taxpayers learn how to escape taxation of income from other sources.[8]

Many countries, especially in the industrial world, allow fast write-offs for investment expenditures—either all investments or those they especially want to induce through tax allowances or credits.[9] Investment tax allowances have distinct advantages. The incentive is correctly targeted at the desired activity since a company receives the benefit of lower corporate taxes only if it makes capital investments (rather than the formation of a new company). It encourages companies to take a long-term view when planning investments. By targeting current capital spending, the allowance causes less rev-

enue leakage than would a tax holiday, and it promotes new investment instead of giving a windfall gain to owners of old capital, as
does a reduction in corporate tax rates. It can also be made refundable, allowing the government to share the investment costs and
risks with the foreign entrepreneur. Still, investment tax allowances
have limitations and drawbacks. If the investment tax allowance is
not refundable, existing companies reap the full benefits (that is,
supporting expansion), while start-up companies must first earn
enough income to be able to take the allowance. Also, projects with
long gestation periods suffer in comparison with those that begin
earning income quickly. When inflation is high, the allowance aggra-
vates the tax system's uneven impact on the investment behavior of
companies. Companies in high-inflation countries will benefit more
if they borrow to finance capital, because tax deductions for capital
expenditures are more valuable. This is the reverse of tax holidays and
of lower corporate tax rates, which reduce the advantages of interest-
cost deductions for tax purposes during high inflation.

Finally, an extreme approach is to reduce or simply eliminate taxes
to all or specific investors. Some countries have become tax havens,
especially in the Caribbean and Pacific regions. They generally choose
to suppress all direct income taxes and rely on indirect consumption
and employment taxes. Other countries have limited these benefits
to specific areas and export-oriented activities—the so-called export
processing zones (EPZs). These zones usually provide a number of
benefits to firms that export a minimum share of total output (usually more than 70–80 percent). In virtually all of these zones, there
is a tax holiday for a substantial period of time (often 10 years),
coupled with a reduction or elimination of import taxes on machinery and production inputs. In addition, the zones usually provide
less cumbersome procedures for importing and exporting.

Tax haven countries are successful in encouraging FDI, but this
has to be qualified because they principally attract mobile companies or activities that are relatively global, such as banking, insurance, and Internet companies. Today, the Cayman Islands claims to
be the fifth-largest financial center, as it is home to subsidiaries of

45 of the world's largest banks. It has to be noted that tax havens are much less successful in convincing multinational firms to relocate their corporate headquarters than to establish new subsidiaries, partly reflecting the tax and regulatory costs of doing so from the home countries (Collins and Shackelford 1995). The experience with EPZs has been mixed, as reported by Magati (1999). It remains unclear if the benefits (employment, exports) outweigh the costs (foregone tax revenues, distortions in the allocation of resources). In many countries, such regimes have created a dichotomy between EPZ companies and those operating under the common regime. The capacity of customs and tax administrations to properly manage and control EPZ companies has also been a crucial element in the performance of EPZs.

4

Issues in Today's Global World

In recent years, the globalization process and the gradual elimination of barriers to capital movements, including FDI, across countries have led to the emergence of new issues. The first issue to receive growing attention from researchers is the interaction between the home and host countries' taxation regimes and its resulting impact on FDI flows. Second, the issue of tax competition between countries and across regions is also widely debated in view of the growing importance of this phenomenon worldwide. Finally, several highly publicized recent deals reveal that a few multinational companies have received large, perhaps disproportionate, tax rebates, which suggests that the costs—not only the benefits—of tax incentives need to be examined more closely. These three issues are reviewed below.

Home Country Tax Policy

In the presence of international capital mobility, home country corporate income tax rates and rules about how taxes paid in the host country are considered at home should influence FDI. In fact, such influence was recognized a long time ago by the bilateral agreements that were signed to avoid double taxation of income between countries (see UNCTAD 1995). The current literature emphasizes two additional effects: (1) the influence of the home country's tax system on the efficacy of the tax incentives granted by the host country, and (2) its impact on the way multinationals do business abroad.

The home country's taxation rules have an impact on the effectiveness of tax incentives in the host country. Most FDI outflows originate from members of the Organisation for Economic Cooperation and Development (OECD), with different regimes on how they tax the activities of their multinationals abroad. For example, the foreign tax paid by U.S. companies can be claimed as a tax credit on U.S. tax liabilities (up to a rate of 35 percent). Japan and the United Kingdom use similar tax credit systems, while other countries—such as Australia, Canada, France, Germany, and the Netherlands—exempt, more or less, any profits earned abroad from home taxation. In 1996, Hines compared the distribution of FDI within the United States of foreign investors whose home governments grant foreign tax credits for federal income and state income taxes with those whose governments do not tax income earned in the United States. His findings reveal that companies with home country tax-free rules (such as France and Canada) have more invested in low-tax states than do those that have to pay taxes in their home countries (Japan and the United Kingdom).[10] A more recent study by the same author (Hines 1998) found that Japanese firms have a tendency to favor investment in countries where Japan has agreements to claim foreign tax credits for income taxes that they would have paid to foreign governments in the absence of tax holidays.[11] From a policy perspective, these two findings seem to indicate that tax incentives are more effective when they apply to firms from countries whose governments do not tax their foreign activities.

Some recent evidence shows that the home country's taxation system is likely to influence the way their multinational companies do business abroad. Hines and Hubbard (1990) and Grubert (1998) found that it is attractive for U.S. firms to use debt to finance foreign investment in high-tax countries (compared with the United States) and equity in low-tax countries. The argument is that the debt generates interest deductions for the subsidiary and so reduces its taxable income in the host country (note that the parent firm has to pay additional taxes, but at a lower rate, in the United States). Harris (1993) uses firm-level data to illustrate that the Tax Reform Act of 1986 in the United States pushed U.S. firms with higher equipment/structure ratios to invest abroad more heavily because their tax regime encouraged such an action. A series of other recent studies have found similar results for preferred-stock issuances (Collins and Shackelford 1997) or domestic versus foreign borrowing (Atshuler and Mintz 1995). An interesting finding is that the 1986 tax reform also influences the form of business organization that the multinational will select in the foreign country. For example, since 1986, American investors have had fewer tax incentives to participate in joint ventures, particularly in low-tax foreign countries, and the number for this type of foreign investment fell sharply, as reported by Desai and Hines (1999).

Finally, the importance of the home country tax system can also be illustrated by the efforts of tax authorities to prevent the transfer of multinationals' headquarters or other specific activities (such as research and development) to other countries. Many governments negotiate contractual arrangements or, and often simultaneously, impose high penalties if the multinational company decides to make such moves. For example, the costs of transferring a parent company, if it is already incorporated in the United States, are prohibitive because the tax administration generally takes the view that the firm is selling off its assets, and levies a substantial capital gains tax. On the other hand, the U.S. tax system provides incentives to local R and D if imported technology and local technology are substitutes, and thus discourages U.S. firms from moving those activities abroad (see Hines 1999).

Harmonization versus Tax Competition

In recent years, there has been new empirical evidence that tax rates and incentives influence the location decisions of companies within regional economic groupings, such as the European Union and those created by the North American Free Trade Agreement and the Association of Southeast Asian Nations (ASEAN). The location decisions of foreign companies within the United States have also commanded the attention of several researchers (Ondrich and Wasylenko 1993 and Swensson 1994). As an illustration of this effect, Devereux and Griffith (1998) found that the average effective tax rate plays a significant role in the choice of U.S. companies to locate within Europe. This factor, however, does not seem to influence the choice of whether to locate in Europe compared with one of the outside options (domestic or other foreign markets).

Such findings confirm the idea that was put forward by Forsyth (1972) about 30 years ago. The potential effectiveness of fiscal incentives is that they are able to make a difference between competing jurisdictions in which the basic, more important conditions, in other words the fixed locational characteristics, are more or less equivalent. These jurisdictions may be subnational or in different countries included in a supranational unified market (such as the European Union). Here, once a locational decision is narrowed down to a handful of alternative sites, incentives can play a decisive role in the final choice.

Since tax policy seems to have a greater impact on the location decision within regional markets, the argument is that it can push governments to "race to the bottom" with competitive tax reductions. The main concern is that the various countries may end up in a bidding war that results in a "prisoner's dilemma" that benefits the foreign firms at the expense of the winning state and the welfare of its citizens.

The issue of tax competition across countries or regions has led to many studies in the past few years. For example, Haaparanta (1996) shows that countries will engage in a tax-bidding process to attract FDI if their key motivation is to create jobs. The same reasoning can apply to R and D. Hauffer and Wooton (1999) suggest that the size of the host country may also matter. In principle, countries with large domestic markets are capable of taxing more FDI because they benefit from positive agglomeration effects, but this advantage decreases with lower trade costs, as it may happen in regional groupings and trade unions. Overall, the outcome of tax competition is generally ambiguous because it depends on many factors, such as the following: Do governments enter into cooperative or noncooperative contests? Do firms operate in a competitive or noncompetitive market? What kinds of tax instruments do the governments use?

In reality, it is difficult to assess the magnitude of tax competition across countries or within a country because of the inherent difficulty of obtaining any reliable data from governments and even more so from firms (see Oman 2000 for a tentative assessment in several countries and regions). Tax competition seems to be more intensive in some sectors, such as automotive, and for larger firms. In any case, both the European Union and OECD have declared that tax competition is harmful to countries. However, this view has to be contrasted with the argument that variations in tax regimes are a good thing because they give taxpayers more choice, and thus more chance of being satisfied, as well as some pressure on governments to compete by offering different combinations of public services and taxes.

Recent efforts to harmonize tax systems have been launched in both the industrial and developing worlds. For example, it has been one of the major objectives of the European Union, in which member countries are discussing more stable, predictable, and transparent tax rules for investors and governments alike. A first step was achieved in December 1997 with the adoption of the Code of Conduct for business taxation in which member states agree not to introduce "harmful" tax measures and to roll back existing harmful measures. Similarly, several West African countries have been undertaking a joint effort to harmonize their tax incentives for FDI in one unified investment code within the Monetary Union of West African States. These processes have been slow and the challenge remains great at both the political and economic levels. The fact of the matter is that the temptation to use tax incentives for attracting FDI will certainly increase as a consequence of the growing mobility of capital and companies across countries and regions, as well as the homogenization of basic fundamentals across (larger) economic areas.

The Costs of Fiscal Incentives

The debate about the effectiveness of incentives in attracting investment—the potential benefit side—has diverted attention from the cost side. Even if tax incentives were quite effective in increasing investment flows, the costs might well outweigh the benefits. This issue has become critical in view of the increase in tax competition around the world. This competition is not only taking place in relatively wealthy industrial countries but also in emerging markets, where governments generally face severe budgetary constraints.[12]

There is no doubt that tax incentives are costly. The first and most direct costs are those associated with the potential loss of revenues for the host government.[13] The effort here is to determine whether the new foreign investment would have come to the country if no or lower incentives were offered. In such cases, "free rider" investors benefit, but the Treasury loses, and there are no net benefits to the economy. An interesting recent study of the state of South Carolina in the United States (Figlio and Blonigen 1999) shows that foreign direct investment has several important negative impacts on the state budget, in fact more than new domestic investment. Not only did they generate more revenue losses (an average-size new foreign firm is associated with a 1.2 percent reduction in real per capita revenues, while a domestic firm, only 0.1 percent) but also additional expenses on infrastructure and education, even though these may have indirect benefits for the economy. These results simply illustrate that attracting foreign companies is not a "zero-sum game" from a public finance perspective.

Tax policy and incentives have many, perhaps less evident, additional costs. Indeed, the argument for their efficacy presupposes that tax authorities are capable of identifying the "positive externalities" of investments, and determining the exact level of tax incentives required to attract the investor. Most incentive programs have relied on vague assessments of potential externalities, and presumptions of policymakers about both the desirability and likelihood of attracting certain types of investments.[14] The distortional effects of incentives on the allocation of resources can be significant, as they bias the investment decisions of private companies. Incentives can be further counterproductive if they contribute to attracting more investors of the "wrong kind," which is certainly the case in countries where basic services are not yet in place.

Another problem with incentive measures relates less to whether they achieve their objectives than to the difficulty and cost of administering them effectively. Put another way, incentive regimes generally impose a significant administrative burden and must therefore be more than marginally effective in order to cover the costs of implementing them, and they must produce a net overall benefit. On this point, it is worth mentioning the difference between discretionary regimes, which depend upon case by case evaluations, and nondiscretionary regimes, which grant incentives to whatever company meets clearly stated requirements. Difficult-to-administer discretionary regimes result in delays and uncertainty for investors, which can even increase the overall cost of making an investment in some countries. They have also been significant sources of corruption, effectively screening out desirable investment, and detrimental to the processes of developing competitive markets and sound policymaking. In contrast, automatic incentive regimes are easier to implement, and generally involve such incentives as investment tax credits, accelerated depreciation, and subsidies linked to indicators that can easily be measured (exports, technology imports, skilled labor). One has to keep in mind, however, that successful examples such as Singapore and Ireland are rare. There have been more governments that failed to attract FDI with targeted tax incentives, explaining why the recent trend has been to eliminate and streamline tax incentive programs. In fact, it seems that multinationals place more importance on simplicity and stability in the tax system than on generous tax rebates, especially in an environment with great political and institutional risks (see Ernst & Young 1994).

5

Concluding Remarks and Next Steps

In summary, incentives will generally neither make up for serious deficiencies in the investment environment nor generate the desired externalities. Thus, advisers often counsel long-run strategies of improving human and physical infrastructure and, where necessary, streamlining government policies and procedures, thereby increasing the chances of attracting investment on a genuine long-term basis. Indeed, the importance of such fundamental factors as economic conditions and political climate is underlined by the fact that the most serious investors are often unaware of the full range of incentives on offer when they invest, and that they often do not consider alternative locations.

Recent evidence has nevertheless shown that when factors such as political and economic stability, infrastructure, and transport costs are more or less equal between potential locations, taxes may exert a significant impact. This is evidenced by the growing tax competition in regional groupings (such as the European Union) or at the subregional level within one country (such as in the United States). This impact, however, has to be qualified on two important counts.

First, the impact of tax policy may significantly depend on the tax instruments used by the authorities. For example, tax holidays and a general reduction in the statutory tax rate may have an equivalent impact on the effective tax rate but significantly different effects on FDI flows and a government's revenues. Second, the effectiveness of tax policy and incentives is also likely to vary depending on the multinational firm's activity and on its motivations for investing abroad. For example, tax incentives seem to be a crucial factor for mobile firms or firms that operate in multiple markets because they can better exploit the different tax regimes across countries.

The debate swirling around the impact of taxes and fiscal incentives on FDI is far from over. Old questions will lead to new answers, and new questions will emerge. Among all these possibilities, we would like to focus on *five* directions that, we believe, offer ideas for future research. The first direction consists of the eventual nonlinear impact of tax rates on the investment decisions of multinational companies. A look at the reality suggests that countries with excessive tax rates can kill foreign direct investment but those with reasonable tax rates may exert little or no influence on it. At the other extreme, the success of tax haven countries indicates that extremely low tax rates may also attract foreign investors, at least some of them. There is a need for detailed econometric evidence of those nonlinear effects, as they may have implications for policymakers who wish to use tax policy to attract foreign investors.

The second direction for research could be to examine more closely the effect of tax policy on the composition of FDI (for example, greenfield, reinvested earnings, and mergers and acquisitions). There have been only a few studies on this aspect, most of the authors preferring to focus on the level of total FDI in the country. However, depending on the tax policy or the fiscal incentives, foreign investors may choose alternative ways to invest abroad. For example, as mentioned in the previous section, recent changes in U.S. tax policy seem to have discouraged U.S. joint ventures. With a better understanding of how tax policies affect the composition of FDI, policymakers in host countries would have a better chance of attracting the right type of investment and maximizing its impact on the economy.

The third direction is linked to the development of new technologies. As a matter of fact, the Internet has the potential to increase tax competition, not least by making it much easier for multinationals to shift their activities to low-tax regimes that are physically a long way from their customers but are virtually only a mouse-click away. As reported in Globalization (2000), "many more companies may be able to emulate Rupert Murdoch's News Corporation, which has earned profits of US$2.3 billion in Britain since 1987 but paid no corporation tax there." The emergence of global companies will have a significant impact on government revenues. These companies are more likely to be sensitive to tax incentives because they will be more capable of exploiting them by transferring their activities from one country to another. Additional evidence is certainly needed on this rapidly expanding sector of the economy.

The fourth direction concerns the need for a global approach to the taxation of multinational companies. Within that vision, the following questions merit further attention: (1) Should countries harmonize their tax regimes, and if yes, how? (2) Should transfer pricing or other techniques used by multinational companies to exploit cross-country differences in tax regimes be restricted? (This practice was adopted recently by U.S. tax legislators, who can force companies to repatriate their profits if authorities believe that they are attempting to avoid taxation.) (3) Should a global agency calculate the profit of a multinational company worldwide and then allocate it to an individual country on the basis of a formula that reflects the firm's presence in that country? Today, these areas offer more questions than answers, but it has to be recognized that a global approach is increasingly needed because national boundaries are fading away and national tax administrations are losing their control over taxpayers.

The fifth direction lies in the question, Should tax incentives be directed only at (foreign) investors who make the "right things" in the host country, such as environment-safe projects, or those leading to employment or transfers of technology and marketing skills? This new trend caught the attention of a few researchers in the past couple of years. For example, Markusen et al. (1995) study a model in which governments compete through environmental taxes when productive activity causes local pollution (see also Rauscher 1995). Hines (1999) found that American-owned foreign affiliates are more R and D intensive if located in countries that impose high withholding taxes on royalty payments, and similarly, that foreign firms investing in the United States are more R and D intensive if they are subject to higher royalty withholding taxes. Recently, Blonigen and Slaughter (1999) suggest that tax policy influences the number of foreign affiliates that use skilled labor and transfer new technologies in the host country. These recent studies indicate that tax policy can be used not only to attract foreign investors but also to regulate some of their activities in the host economy. This issue merits further research, especially as there is a need for additional evidence of these possible effects at both the country and enterprise levels.

Notes

1. According to Wells (1999), the earliest reference was in 1160, when wool weavers were offered tax incentives to locate in Biella, in the Piedmont region of Northern Italy.

2. In the *Fortune*/Deloitte Touche survey, taxes ranked 13th out of 26 factors.

3. There exists considerable literature on this concept, which include recent developments such as uncertainty, relations between labor and capital taxes, and indirect taxes. Several studies can be found in Anwar Shah (1995).

4. The average rate can be viewed as the marginal rate multiplied by the statutory average tax rate.

5. It has to be noted that in principle the location decision of the firm may be affected by the marginal and average rates in two opposite directions. When the average level is high in one country, it is possible that the overall profit level may be less than in another country even though its marginal rate is lower.

6. For his study, Reuber separated investors into different groups according to their type of investment (market seeking or export oriented). He used 80 investment projects in various industries of 30 developing countries, made by companies from various national origins. The companies

surveyed were asked to identify, among various incentives, which one was deemed so important that its absence would have caused the abandonment of the project or major changes in it. Among export-oriented projects, 48 percent named fiscal incentives (including tax holidays, duty remission, and accelerated depreciation). Among market-oriented projects, 56 percent of responses named protection of the market as the prevailing factor. By using a different approach to define the problem, Reuber (1973) shows that investment incentives may not matter to all investors, but they do matter to some investors having a specific investment strategy (for example, export platform). Another merit of the study is to pose the question, Do incentives matter? in terms of the location of the projects rather than a broader decision to carry out FDI.

7. For example, an effective tax rate in the United States of about 25 percent at the end of 1994 was produced by a 38 percent corporate tax rate combined with no investment tax allowance, depreciation rates of 4.4 percent on buildings and 18.6 percent on machinery, and a number of other assumptions about inflation, interest rates (interest is deductible), and so forth. Approximately the same effective tax rate was achieved in Spain with a lower corporate tax rate (35 percent) and lower rates of depreciation on buildings (3 percent) and equipment (12 percent).

8. For example, during the holiday years, companies operate at a preferential corporate tax rate. When corporate taxpayers have a choice, they have an incentive to shift income into a company enjoying the tax holiday and take more deductible expenses in another company they may own that must pay taxes. They would prefer to have the taxpaying company incur interest costs on borrowed finances and the tax holiday company to be financed with equity. In fact, the tax holiday company could hold debt in the non-holiday company. The non-holiday company can deduct interest while the tax-holiday company earns the interest tax-free.

9. These allowances take three forms: (1) accelerated depreciation, which allows companies to write off capital more quickly for tax purposes than for accounting; (2) an investment expenditure allowance that lets companies write off a percentage of qualifying investment expenditures from their taxable income; and (3) an investment tax credit that allows companies to reduce taxes paid by a percentage of investment expenditures.

10. Note that Slemrod (1990) did not find any clear pattern at the country (rather than the state) level.

11. Hines shows that Japanese firms are subject to 23 percent lower tax rates than are their American counterparts in countries with whom Japan has agreements. In other words, Japanese firms have a greater propensity to invest when they can benefit from tax incentives than when they cannot because they would have to pay taxes in Japan.

12. This is certainly the main argument used when tax incentives are frequently eliminated in a budgetary crisis; see recent examples of East Asian countries (for example, Indonesia), as discussed by Wells (1999).

13. It is estimated that the direct and indirect fiscal "cost-per-job" of incentives received by investors in the automobile industry often exceeds US$100,000 (see Oman 2000).

14. Even if incentives are effective in attracting more investment, the fact is that they distort the profit signals to investors. Thus, unless the envisaged externalities can somehow be generated, the resources used by a government to fund incentive measures are being put to less than optimal use.

References

Agodo, O. 1978. "The Determinants of U.S. Private Manufacturing Invest-ments in Africa." *Journal of International Business Studies* 9: 95–107.

Aharoni, Y. 1966. *The Foreign Investment Decision Process.* Cambridge, Mass.: Harvard University Press.

Atshuler, R., and J. Mintz. 1995. "U.S. Interest-Allocation Rules: Effects and Policy." *International Tax and Public Finance* 2 (1): 7–35.

Barlow, E., and I. Wender. 1955. *Foreign Investment and Taxation.* Englewood Cliffs: Prentice Hall.

Blonigen, B., and M. Slaughter. 1999. "Foreign-Affiliate Activity and U.S. Skill Upgrading." National Bureau of Economic Research Working Pa-per 7040. Cambridge, Mass.

Bond, E., and L. Samuelson. 1986. "Tax Holidays as Signals." *The Ameri-can Economic Review* 76(4): 820–26.

Boskin, M., and W. Gale. 1987. "New Results on the Effects of Tax Policy on the International Location of Investment." In M. Feldstein, ed., *The Effects of Taxation on Capital Accumulation.* Chicago: University of Chicago Press.

Collins, J., and D. Shackelford. 1995. "Corporate Domicile and Average Effective Tax Rates: The Cases of Canada, Japan, the United King-dom, and the United States." *International Tax and Public Finance* 2(1): 55–83.

Collins, J., and D. Shackelford. 1997. "Global Organizations and Taxes: An Analysis of the Dividend, Interest, Royalty, and Management Fee Payments between U.S. Multinationals' Foreign Affiliates." *Journal of Accounting and Economics* 24: 151–73.

Coyne, E. J. 1994. "An Articulated Analysis Model for FDI Attraction into Developing Countries." M.B.A. thesis. Nova Southeastern University, Fort Lauderdale, Fla.

Desai, M., and J. Hines. 1999. "Basket Cases: Tax Incentives and International Joint Venture Participation by American Multinational Firms." *Journal of Public Economics* 71(3): 379–402.

Devereux, M., and R. Griffith. 1998. "Taxes and the Location of Production: Evidence from a Panel of U.S. Multinationals." *Journal of Public Economics* 68: 335–67.

Ernst & Young. 1994. "Investment in Emerging Markets: A Survey of the Strategic Investment of Global 1000 Companies." New York.

Figlio, D., and B. Blonigen. 1999. "The Effects of Direct Foreign Investment on Local Communities." National Bureau of Economic Research Working Paper 7274. Cambridge, Mass.

Forsyth, D. 1972. *U.S. Investment in Scotland*. New York: Praeger.

Fortune/Deloitte Touche. 1997. "1997 Business Location Study." Processed.

"Globalization and Tax." 2000. *The Economist,* Jan. 29: 7–22.

Group of Thirty. 1992. *Foreign Direct Investment: 1973–87.* New York: Group of Thirty.

Grubert, H. 1998. "Taxes and the Division of Foreign Operating Income among Royalties, Interest, Dividends, and Retained Earnings." *Journal of Public Economics* 68 (2): 285–93.

Grubert, H., T. Goodspeed, and D. Swensson. 1993. "Explaining the Low Taxable Income of Foreign-Controlled Companies in the U.S." In A. Giovannini, R. Hubbard, and J. Slemrod, eds., *Studies in International Taxation*. Chicago: University of Chicago Press, 1993.

Guisinger, S. and others. 1985. *Investment Incentives and Performance Requirements.* New York: Praeger.

Haaparanta, P. 1996. "Competition for Foreign Direct Investment." *Journal of Public Economics* 63: 141–53.

Harris, D. 1993. "The Impact of U.S. Tax Law Revision on Multinational Corporations' Capital Location and Income-Shifting Decisions." *Journal of Accounting Research* 31: 111–40. Supplement.

Hartman, D. 1985. "Tax Policy and Foreign Direct Investment." *Journal of Public Economics* 26 (1): 107–21.

Hauffer, A., and I. Wooton. 1999. "Country Size and Tax Competition for Foreign Direct Investment." *Journal of Public Economics* 71: 121–39.

Hines, J. 1996. "Altered States: Taxes and the Location of Foreign Direct Investment in America." *American Economic Review* 86 (5): 1076–94.

———. 1998. " 'Tax Sparing' and Direct Investment in Developing Countries." National Bureau of Economic Research Working Paper 6728. Cambridge, Mass.

———. 1999. "Lessons from Behavioral Responses to International Taxation." *National Tax Journal* 52(2): 305–22.

Hines, J., and G. Hubbard. 1990. "Coming Home to America: Dividend Repatriations by U.S. Multinationals." In A. Razin and J. Slemrod, eds., *Taxation in the Global Economy*. Chicago: University of Chicago Press.

Japan External Trade Organization (JETRO). 1995. "The Current State of Japanese Affiliated Manufacturers in ASEAN—1994." Tokyo: Overseas Research Department.

Lim, D. 1983. "Fiscal Incentives and Direct Foreign Investment in Less Developed Countries." *Journal of Development Studies* 19(2): 207–12.

Magati, D. 1999. "A Review of the Role and Impact of Export Processing Zones." World Bank, Development Research Group, Trade. Washington, D.C.

Markusen, J. R., E. Morey, and N. Olewiler. 1995. "Competition in Regional Environment Policies When Plant Locations Are Endogenous." *Journal of Public Economics* 56: 55–77.

Mintz, J., and T. Tsiopoulos. 1992. "Corporate Income Taxation and Foreign Direct Investment." Foreign Investment Advisory Service Occasional Paper 4. World Bank, Washington, D.C.

Oman, C. 2000. "Policy Competition for Foreign Direct Investment: A Study of Competition among Governments to Attract FDI." OECD Development Centre Studies, Paris.

Ondrich, J., and M. Wasylenko. 1993. *Foreign Direct Investment in the United States: Issues, Magnitudes, and Location Choice of New Manufacturing Plants.* Kalamazoo, Mich.: W.E. Upjohn Institute.

Rauscher, M. 1995. "Environment Regulation and the Location of Polluting Industries." *International Tax and Public Finance* 2: 229–44.

Reuber, G. 1973. *Private Foreign Investment in Development.* Oxford, Eng.: Oxford University Press.

Robinson, H. J. 1961. "The Motivation and Flow of Private Foreign Investment." Stanford Research Institute, Menlo Park, Calif.

Rolfe, R. J., D. Ricks, M. Pointer, and M. McCarthy. 1993. "Determinants of FDI Incentive Preferences of MNEs." *Journal of International Business Studies* 24(2): 335–56.

Root, F., and A. Ahmed. 1978. "The Influence of Policy Instruments on Manufacturing Direct Foreign Investment in Developing Countries." *Journal of International Business Studies* 9(3): 81–93.

Shah, A., ed. 1995. *Fiscal Incentives for Investment and Innovation.* Oxford, Eng.: Oxford University Press.

Shah, S. M., and J. Toye. 1978. "Fiscal Incentives for Firms in Some Developing Countries: Survey and Critique." In J. Toye, ed., *Taxation and Economic Development.* London: Frank Cass.

Slemrod, J. 1990. "Tax Effects on Foreign Direct Investment in the United States: Evidence from a Cross Country Comparison." In A. Razin and J. Slemrod, eds., *Taxation in the Global Economy.* Chicago: University of Chicago Press.

Swensson, D. 1994. "The Impact of U.S. Tax Reform on Foreign Direct Investment in the United States." *Journal of Public Economics* 54: 243–66.

UNCTAD (United Nations Conference on Trade and Development). 1995. "Incentives and Foreign Direct Investment; Background Report." Geneva.

Wells, L. 1986. "Investment Incentives: An Unnecessary Debate." *The CTC Reporter* 22: 58–60.

Wells, L. 1999. "Attracting Foreign Investment: Incentives, Institutions, and Infrastructure." Background paper for the FIAS (Foreign Investment Advisory Service)/UNDP (United Nations Development Programme) High-Level Roundtable, Bangkok.